Out of Uganda in 90 Days

Urmila Patel

Cover designed by Bocheez: www.bocheez.com
Interior design and formatting by ExpertSubjects.com
Author's photo by Nagendra Tiwari

Published by urmila Patel.
For information please Contact Urmila Patel
39632 Paseo Padre pkwy #101
Fremont, CA 94538, USA
Email address: urmila.patel101@yahoo.com
Web: www.OutofUgandain90 days.com
Facebook: facebook.com/urmilapatel57
LinkedIn: www.linkedin.com/pub/urmila-patel/72/808/77/
Twitter: urmila patel@Patelurmila

First printed in the United states of America by Create Space.
ISBN-13:978-1500774295
ISBN-10:1500774294

Dedication

*I dedicate this book to all those who are still haunted by
painful memories from Uganda's upheavals under
Idi Amin. Many individuals and families are still
healing from the hatred and trauma they endured in
those years. Families who had lived for generations
in that land were uprooted and expelled. So many of
these families lost loved ones to violence. Some lived
in refugee camps, learned new languages, and endured
climates they had never experienced. It is for them that
I have written this account.*

About the Author

I was brought up in a Hindu family. From my youngest days, when I first heard the sounds of drums, the priests' mantra chants, and the voices and bells in the temple, I was fascinated and mystified.

Even at the age of 13, I was asking: What is real? What's not? I followed my culture's traditions of prayer and fasting, but as I grew older more questions emerged. What is the deeper meaning of rituals, mantras, and other traditions? What effects do these things have on the human body? Do these traditional methods help us discover the answers that lie within us?

Just over a decade ago, my struggle led me to a fuller understanding of how outside forces can affect us. They follow the law of attraction, influencing our energy and our bodies. This understanding helped explain my fascination with all those sounds. They began a healing process within me, cushioning the effects of unnecessary karma, while freeing my consciousness and energizing my spirit.

I have now reached the moment when it's time to take stock, see the whole of things, and walk the path. I now know that I was born to serve. This is my purpose. I begin with love and passion.

As a Reiki master, I help people. The Reiki energy heals them. With my professional knowledge, I coach them to use their natural strengths to improve their performance and enhance their quality of life. This is the deepest fulfillment I know.

Prologue

From my earliest years I've lived in countries that aren't a part of my family's heritage. I've learned much from other cultures, reading their histories, participating in their traditions, eating their food, and living their lifestyles. I have always felt that I was free to observe these traditions without being bound by them. This is the beauty of oneself.

I grew up in what seemed like a paradise in Uganda. In this East African nation we lived amidst mountains, lakes, forests and jungles. Adding beauty to all of this was the tropical weather.

The innocent natives opened their big hearts to us, and helped us see that we were all one. As children we were fearless. We played where we wanted to, in the fields, on the roads and on the edge of the forest. We were as free as birds.

This ended in 1971, when General Idi Amin Dada overthrew President Obote and took power. At that moment our paradise became a hell. Businesses were destroyed, families ruined, people massacred, and girls were dragged from their homes to be raped and killed.

In August of the following year Amin gave all resident Asians 90 days to leave. These events are at the core of my story.

At 14 years of age I wrote my first account of this journey in my little dairy. Though I wasn't sure why I was doing it, I knew that I needed to write down every detail. I was a fully conscious witness. During our escape, while most passengers were asleep, I kept myself awake, not wanting to miss any of the beauty of East Africa and its people.

Now I am a single mother who has raised two children alone. They are both beautiful and intelligent. I brought them up to be independent, well-mannered, and happy. I educated them. They have both graduated, and now they are living their own lives. This is my most treasured gift to myself.

Though I lost my diary, all through the years I've wanted to tell my story to the world. I still vividly recalled our journey, so, in 2000, I began. Other events slowed the progress of writing, but in late 2011 the universe opened doors for me. I finally started writing more and more. Writing healed many of the wounds of family and country.

In 1971 Uganda fell under the rule of a single dictator. Because of him, many of Uganda's people fled, scattering across the globe. Our own home there was ruled by one woman: my mother. My sisters, brother, and I are now scattered. I believe that, had we been able to stay in a peaceful Uganda, this would not have happened.

At this moment, many years later, I wonder what my mother was going through during that time. I now have a better understanding of all my family was enduring, as we faced fear, intolerance, and potentially fatal violence. The wounds we suffered were bound to come back later as illnesses of different kinds.

How did it happen? When did it start? What was I thinking then? What can I do now to change my thinking? How does that affect generations to come? These questions are at the heart of this story.

I have learned one thing. With the resources of the universe we create the life we want. If we are to live healthy, well-balanced, harmonious, blissful lives we need to take care of ourselves first: inside and out. In this way we can slow down, find peace, enjoy nature, and create a happy, loving world.

Through memories, I am still connected with the many friends and passengers I met on my journey. We all shared the same story.

MY FAMILY:
I am "Mila," and when this story takes place I am 13.
My father is called "Papa." He is 41 in the story.
My mother's name is "Saita", and she is 33.
My sisters are Bina, 15, Donna, 9, and Jaimini, 2. My brother, Kevin, is 6 in the story.

Acknowledgements

A very special thank you to all my readers, all those who I've met on my life's journey, whose lives and experiences have helped me create this book. Sharing my story with you helped me realize just how important it is to surround myself with caring, supportive people. Writing this book helped me reconnect with my dear Ugandan neighbors, colleagues and friends. We have a lot to recapture, old memories to uncover, and we need to see "Where we were and where we are now", as well as what we learned from it.

To my parents for giving me a wonderful childhood: I treasure the good memories within me.

To my son, Amit, who unselfishly allowed me to hibernate so I could complete this project on time. Your sacrifices have not gone unnoticed.

To my daughter Renal for allowing me to see myself in her. You took care of one of the biggest roles— preparing most of your engagement and wedding—and this between your work; taking care of your spoiled dog D'jengo; your on-line classes for higher performance; and your exams; giving me enough space to concentrate on my writing. You are an example to many. I am blessed to have had you come into my life.

To Dr Charleen Rocha: I accept you as a dear part of my family. You took time from your busy schedule to help me create a website for this book.

To my sisters and brother for giving me the wonderful memories.

To Jana Andres, a leadership coach and colleague, you helped me dig out the message for this book, which lay deep within myself.

To a wonderful friend, Adassa, who I met six years back. Your serenity and radiated energy helped me understand that there is something greater beyond just the daily humdrum of human life. You stayed close to my process when I started writing, and created a very pleasant time while proofreading. I am grateful to have met a friend like you.

To Jeff lamei. With your powerful healing knowledge, you helped me uncover and release the troubles that had pressured me for so long. Through you and Clara, a great spiritual Native American woman, I reconnected with my ancient Vedic knowledge.

To Linda Coleman. You and your book "for self publishing authors" have been a great help to me in finding great ideas.

Many thanks to the country of Belgium, its generous people and the Caritas Catholica for their tremendous sympathy and support. This was the country that took my father as a refugee.

To Susie, Amber and Bonnie, my loyal employees. You have been a great help in keeping my business stable during my absence. You ladies are awesome!

To Peter Heyrman and everyone at Bear press. Peter, your expertise and creative suggestions are invaluable. With your great help editing and final proofreading, this book took shape and became alive to the world.

To Mike Barth for proofing and Sally Miller for final proofing.

"To Greg Kihn, an American rock musician and novelist: thank you for your generosity in referring me to your friend and editor Peter, Heyrman. Greg, I am blessed to have a friend like you."

"Cover designed by Bocheez. Thank you for your patience working with me. I know it was a challenge as I made you go back and forth for days, adding and deleting details.

To all my colleagues, my clients at Postal Annex, family, friends and acquaintances. Your enthusiasm while waiting to read my book helped keep me excited moving forward with this project.

To the Indian community of Kenya, I thank you for your generosity. The warm meal and warm blankets you provided kept us warm and alive.

To each and everyone who I might have forgotten to mention in creating this book, thank you.

All my Love and devotion to the higher self, who guides me in all things, and helps me walk my path with Love and Light.

OUT OF UGANDA IN 90 DAYS, is the story of Idi Amin's ruthless short lived dictatorship over the "Pearl of Africa". This story is told from the viewpoint of a spirited little girl of East Indian descent.

Her family dynamics; a Mother a Father, Brother and Sisters. Religion and faith their bond...which ultimately prevailed in a time of adventure, wonder & danger.

The pure inner child which hopefully resides within us all. Her account fills us with a real and tangible meaning of God's Grace Mercy and Goodness which verily endures forever.

The timbre of the native Swahili tongue viscerally soothes and heals.

This memoir speaks of "The Cradle of Civilization"-rocked by envy, greed, violence and spiritual wickedness in high places.

Indigenous people powerless against brutality enforced by guns knives and sticks.

The miracle is not only that her life was spared but that the author is not a

hatemonger. She has transcended the prejudice the hatred and learned behavior which could so easily have beset her and bound her eternal spirit.

Urmila holds forgiveness and hope in her heart for world peace and unity.

By Pauline Elaine Adassa

A MEMOIR
BY
URMILA PATEL

Table of Contents

CHAPTER 1
Kampala, 1972

So we said good-bye to our father.

It was one pm. The guard blew the third whistle and the train moved slowly out of the station. Papa walked alongside the train, holding our hands, as he told Mum: "Don't worry about me. I will reunite with you as soon as I can."

He then released our hands. Kevin and I stuck our heads out the train window. We kept waving. On the receding platform, Papa got smaller and smaller, until we could no longer see him.

The train jerked and roared forward. The movement thrilled me, and I began taking deep breaths. As I exhaled, I felt as if I were expelling all the horrors I'd experienced during those last months and days in Kampala. The train took on speed. Wind blew in. There, at the window, I rested my head on my hands, closed my eyes, and inhaled the fresh air. As I grew sleepy, my mind went back months, to my earliest memories of trouble.

Earlier, in our home:

I could recall waking up to the familiar sounds of singing birds and our neighbor's cock crowing. I hadn't needed an alarm clock. Mum was already awake, timing her house chores to the minute. With seven in the family, her cooking, cleaning and washing never seemed to end. On weekends and vacations my older sister, Bina, and I helped, giving Mum enough time to concentrate on her other work.

Bina and I had learned to make tea and roti (an Indian bread). For lunch Mum made authentic Gujarati food with fresh vegetables, lentil soup, rice and the rotis. On special occasions there were extra side dishes and desserts.

The roti took a lot of time. Bina always rolled while I baked. I would watch carefully as Bina placed her hands on both sides of the rolling pin, giving it soft pressure. As she moved her hands from right to left, the dough would spread wider and wider, taking a round shape. My shapes never came out round. When I rolled, there were always thinner and thicker parts.

I recalled a Sunday morning after Bina had gotten a small cut on her hand while harvesting sugar cane. When this stopped her from rolling the dough, I offered to do it.

"Oh, no," she said. "You don't know how to roll them round."

"I will try," I insisted, and I started rolling.

Bina looked on, saying, "Oh! Which continent did you make?"

"It's India," I said and we both laughed. I attempted two rotis before Bina intervened. She'd ignored her cut, taking over. We had a clay stove so small that we could carry it into the living room and bake while watching our favorite show: Bonanza.

Our dinner was usually either some Indian specialty, or fresh fruits from the garden. Mum was a very good cook. She made sure there were enough homemade snacks the whole year round.

Bina helped Mum with the housework, and with the care of our 2-year-old sister, Jaimini. Bina preferred housework to school. She found school boring, and Mum loved it when my sister did the chores.

Mum owned a small convenience store on the hospital field. When she'd tired of carrying her growing Jaimini to work, she'd started looking for someone who could babysit the 2-year-old. An African customer suggested his 14-year-old niece, Tiko, for the job.

"Oh yes," the man had said, "my niece is at home. She will gladly help you. She is a very good girl. She will obey you. She will also take good care of your baby. I will bring her tomorrow morning."

The next morning Tiko had arrived, greeting Mum in Swahili. "Hujambo,"

"Hujambo," Mum replied. Mum began telling Tiko her duties. "You have to carry my baby, Jaimini, and walk with me to my work during the week. At home, you will have to clean the dishes, and feed, wash and watch Jaimini. Can you do all that?"

"Ndiyo, Mama," Tiko replied, saying "yes" in her language.

But Mum's customer had been wrong about his niece. Tiko was a cold person, who'd turned out to be careless and lazy. She'd done very little work. On weekends she spent most of her time sitting in the back yard, her hands raised to her temples.

One day Mum sniffed the air, and asked: "What's that horrible smell?" Suspecting Jaimini's nappy, Mum checked it, and found it needed changing. "Tiko," Mum called, but she got no answer.

Tiko had fallen asleep.

When Mum saw this, she raised her voice: "Tiko, why didn't you change Jaimini's nappy?" she asked. She spoke to the girl in Swahili: "Kwanini wewe kubadili jamini wa winda?"

"I did," Tiko claimed, rubbing sleep from her eyes.

"No, you did not. Go wash her. Right now!"

Tiko did not move.

"Jaimini needs to be washed," Mum repeated.

Tiko rose slowly from her chair, picked up Jaimini, and took her into the bathroom. She put Jaimini's butt under the running water and cleaned her.

Later Mum had told Papa: "I'm so tired of telling Tiko what she's supposed to do."

"She's immature," said Papa, "but at least she carries Jamini for you. You complained about that. How will you manage without her?"

"I will manage," said Mum, "but I don't want to lose any more of my energy."

Finally Mum spoke to the girl, saying: "Tiko, here are your shillings. I do not want you to come to work anymore." Tiko walked away sadly.

We lived in a small, freestanding house of about 1,200 square feet. It had two small rooms, a kitchen, a bathroom and a hallway. The living room and kitchen faced northeast, where a huge mango tree blocked the morning sun. During the day this was perfect. The tree branches covered a quarter of the roof, which gave coolness to the living room and kitchen.

In the afternoons the sun shone on the backyard, heating the master bedroom. Because of that we always kept the master bedroom window closed during the daytime. Mornings brought fresh scents from the forest, and as water dripped from the tree leaves onto the grass, I would feel at peace. As the sun rose, the moisture on the roads evaporated, and the world seemed to rejuvenate itself. Patches of night fog on trimmed grass broke up as we passed through them, or disintegrated in the sunlight. Mum said an early morning barefoot walk on the grass brought good luck.

Our Papa didn't argue about small details, usually keeping quiet. Papa was 5'9", had an athletic build, a strong constitution, dark curly hair and dark brown eyes. He was quiet, had great knowledge, and we all respected his words. He was disciplined, brave, open-minded and had great ideas. One thing was missing; he was not handy.

We were all afraid of Mum. She was small, athletic and multi-talented, and she had a powerful resilient energy. She was hardworking and preferred to earn the respect of others, rather than ask for it. She was determined and able to persevere in the face of adversity. She liked to be busy. She didn't show emotions easily, and stayed within her small domain.

Industrious and conscientious, Mum could not take no for an answer. She wanted things done her way. Her short temper sometimes flared out of control, and she would beat us for our mistakes. She had her own goodness, and expected perfection from all of us at all times. She had no time for "flakiness" or unreliability in others. She was hard on herself.

Mum's small sharp eyes seemed to take in everything in a single glance. She was creative, and sewed for outsiders, as well as for the family. The dresses she made for us were stylish and fashionable, with the latest prints. If she started a dress, she would not go to sleep until it was finished. Bina would get a new dress first, followed by me, then with whatever material was left over, she sewed for Donna. Later, she sewed men's suits and trousers. Papa was glad.

CHAPTER 2

We loved our mango tree. It gave us fruit and much more. In our spare time we often played a board game called Lido in the shade of that tree. We were always careful not to wake Papa from his afternoon nap. If he saw us unoccupied, he'd tell us to study for school, or read a book.

During the season the tree's limbs were loaded with small mangoes. Most were the size of walnuts. They had a sweet taste when ripe. We used the unripe ones to make mango pickles. Mum conserved them in a big jar filled with pickle masala and oil. The hardest part about mangoes was harvesting. To get them down off the tree we could wait for a big storm to do the work for us, or we could ask one of the neighbor's boys to do it. One boy, Enoks Asiimwe, was a very good climber and knew how to climb huge trees. We called him "Tarzan."

One evening, when Mum was watering the flowers in the front yard, she put down the water can and looked up. "Ah ha," she said to herself, while scratching her head. "This year, the mangoes are two weeks early—still green and just the right size for pickles." Her brow furrowed as she considered this. "Who will climb the tree?" she wondered. "May be Enoks. He's stubborn. I will go to his house and ask him." She recalled that the year before he'd gone up in the tree, but before he shook the branch, his Mum had called him. He'd run home, leaving her with no mangoes. Fortunately there had been a huge storm later that week, scattering enough mangoes for a single jar. This year she wanted to make enough to last a whole year.

"Bina," Mum called, "pack me some homemade snacks."

"Where are you going, Mum?" Bina asked.

"To Enoks's house."

"Why?"

"To ask him to get some mangoes for me."

Bina packed up the snacks, and Mum went off on her mission.

"Enoks, Enoks," Mum called, as she approached his house.

The boy's mother appeared. She was a tall shiny-skinned woman, wearing a traditional royal blue dress with printed white flowers, and a matching head wrap. "What is it, Madam?" she asked politely in softly spoken Swahili.

"Here," Mum said, handing over the snacks.

"Thank you," said Enoks's mum.

"Could you ask Enoks if he would harvest mangoes for me?" Mum asked.

"I will, Madam," the woman said. "Wait here." She turned into the house. "Enoks?" she called. There was no reply. "Enoks," she called again, her voice firmer this time.

An 11-year-old boy came slowly from his room, head bowed, and his eyes on the door. When he saw our mum he turned to go back, but his mum's voice stopped him.

"Hii si jinsi mimi kufunzeni ya kuishi," she snapped, telling him in Swahili that this was no way to behave.

"What, Mum?" he asked in Swahili.

"This madam wants you to get some mangoes from her tree."

"I'm tired," he protested. "Besides, I have to catch up on my homework."

"Do your homework afterwards," she commanded.

"Sorry, Mum," he said in a low voice. He walked out, his head still bowed.

"My boy has his own mind," his mum said with pride, "but he is obedient."

As they approached our house, Mum pointed at empty buckets and whispered, "I will give you one shilling. I want those two buckets full."

He smiled, his cheeks flushing. He looked up to the branches where the most mangoes were, then started climbing.

"Donna, Kevin," Mum called to my brother and sister, "where are you?" Both children came running. "Here," she said, pointing to the buckets. "Bring these full of mangoes. Make sure not to stand underneath the tree when they're falling. After Enoks shakes them down from the branches, pick them up and fill those buckets. That will be enough for two big jars of pickles—enough to last a year."

Donna and Kevin proudly picked up the buckets and walked to the front yard.

"Mum will be happy with me. My bucket will have more mangoes than yours," Kevin boasted.

Donna raised her dark eyebrows. "My bucket will get full faster than yours," she replied. They began to argue.

Looking out from the living room window, I called: "Stop it!"

When they didn't hear me, I stepped outside, and took away their buckets. "I will only give these back if you two stop arguing," I said.

Suddenly they both stopped, snatched their buckets away from me, and ran.

"Where's Enoks?" I demanded.

Kevin stopped, and pointed up into the tree. "There."

I came closer, but still couldn't see him. "Enoks, Where are you?" I called up into the leafy branches.

"I'm here," he replied, throwing a mango down at me.

"Ouch! That hurts," I cried. I picked up the mango and threw it back at him, but it didn't make it beyond the first branch.

Enoks laughed and sang, "You can't hit me."

"Wait till you come down," I warned as I caught sight of him. He was sitting between the branches, eating a mango. "I can see you," I called up to him. "Eat later. You know Mum. She's waiting for the mangoes. She's already prepared the masala."

Once he was reminded of his reward, Enoks shook the branches as hard as he could. The branches made a sweeping sound as the mangoes fell between them. Small mangoes pelted the grass like stones. I sat on the doorstep, ready with salt and chili, as I watched Donna and Kevin darting about, filling their buckets. They giggled as they gathered, always keeping an eye on each other's bucket.

A branch cracked.

I stood up. "Watch out, Enoks!" I shouted. "Make sure you don't fall."

"Don't shout," he yelled. "You're making me more nervous." He lay, grasping a thick branch. His legs dangled as his butt slipped to the side.

"Watch out!" we shouted.

Mum came outside.

When Enoks saw Mum he pulled himself back up on the branch and started climbing again. I glimpsed scratches on his legs. He climbed higher and higher until we could no longer see any trace of him.

I cut some mangoes in two, removed the seeds, and sprinkled them with salt and chili.

"Yummy, they are crunchy," I said. They tasted delicious, though they were still a little sour. "Come have some, Kevin, Donna."

Kevin's bucket was already full, which upset Donna. "I want my bucket full too," she said. "Mum told me to bring back this bucket full."

"I will help you, I said."

All of 9-years-old, Donna was frightened by anything new. She often played by herself. Though she had her own style and pride, she stubbornly resisted direction from others, and always wanted control. Often she demanded to be boss, but when things didn't work the way she wanted them to, she blamed the people around her. She was sensitive to slights, and easily hurt.

Kevin was our only brother, and had to deal with four sisters. He'd learned to fit in. He was overly expressive, and had a natural exuberance and love of life. He believed anything was possible. He was a mischievous optimist, full of new ideas, and he liked to explore.

If it hadn't been for Enoks, we would have had to wait for a storm. This was when we could collect mangoes with almost no effort. Hard winds threw lots of mangoes all over the grass and onto the roof. The sound of the thunder would be punctuated by the clatter of mangoes on our roof. They sounded like so many rocks. This scared us, especially at night. We thought the mangoes would crash through and hit our heads, so, to be on the safe side, four of us slept together on the bottom of the two-story bed, covering ourselves with the blankets.

There were times when we sat till late in the evenings, holding ourselves together, listening to the sound of the thunder and lighting. The metal roof had no insulation, so it was always cold when it rained.

It was during this time that living in Uganda was becoming more and more impossible for people like us. Idi Amin had taken power the year before, and he had no love for Asians. We would see him on TV, but often the wind blew our antenna, interfering with our reception of the signals. It hardly mattered. His message for us was always the same: though we'd been born in Uganda, he didn't want us to stay. He blamed "foreigners" for the country's problems.

It was a horrible time. Storms had always kept us in, but now there was a different kind of tumult: the violence of Amin's followers. Whether the threat was lightning or human violence, none of us wanted to leave our homes, and only a few fearless neighbors did. As we stayed behind our front door, we could hear the laughing and giggling as others invaded our front yard, taking all the fallen mangoes.

When Mum would check on us during a storm, I would ask her: "Can we go out?"

"No," she would say. "You can't go out. It's too dangerous. Remember what happened to Mr Masaba. I'm afraid a branch would fall upon you or you could be struck by lightning. You can pick some mangoes tomorrow when the storm has gone. There will still be some left for all of you."

Mr. Masaba, his wife, and their son, Moses, had come to our front yard during a heavy storm about a year earlier. As they got their fill of mangoes, Mrs. Masaba grew tired of the battering storm. "Let's go home," she called to her husband and son. "We will come back tomorrow morning." Her son Moses heard her, but Mr. Masaba was too far away, and didn't catch her words. Mrs. Masaba and her son turned to go home, thinking Mr. Masaba would follow. They both ran to get out of the rain and wind.

When a half hour had passed with no let-up in the storm and no sign of her husband, Mrs. Masaba told Moses, "Go, tell your dad to come. Make sure you follow the same path we used coming home."

Moses pushed through the heavy wind and rain, his path lit only by streetlights obscured by the torrents. He could barely see. As he approached our yard, he called, "Dad, Dad, where are you?"

Kevin's sharp ears heard these calls. "Papa," Kevin shouted, "someone is outside. I heard someone calling 'Dad'."

"Oh, yeah," replied Papa, but he didn't take Kevin seriously. The storm was at its worst, and it was hard to imagine anyone would be out in it.

But a few minutes later Kevin said, "Papa, I heard it again."

"I will go check outside," said Papa, taking the torch flashlight and an umbrella. As soon as he unlatched the door, it flew open. Wind-blown rain flew into the living room. Papa stepped outside and pulled the door closed behind him.

"Who are you looking for?" he called into the blustering winds.

"I'm looking for my dad," cried Moses. "He was here with us a little while ago, but when we went home, he didn't follow us."

Thunder crashed above them. It was cold and too dark to see. Papa walked around the yard, shining his light everywhere. "He's not here. Maybe he's gone home."

"But I didn't see him on my way back here," Moses protested.

Papa tried one more time. He walked behind the tree towards the neighbor's fence, pulling off the branches with his stick. He saw something moving. "I found your dad," he called.

Mr. Masaba lay under a big branch. As soon as he saw Papa, he cried out: "Help! I can't move! My leg hurts!"

Seeing his dad lying there, Moses thought he was dead. "Dad! Dad!" he shouted.

"Your dad's still breathing," Papa said. "Here. Hold the umbrella and the torch." When the umbrella blew out of Moses's hands, Papa said: "Let it go. Help me pull the branch away."

They got Mr. Masaba out of there, and dragged him to his house. Mrs. Masaba panicked when she saw the condition of her husband.

"Your husband will regain consciousness soon," Papa told her.

"I will take him to the hospital," Moses volunteered.

Papa shook his head. "It's too risky. Wait till morning. If he's still the same, go to the hospital and ask for the ambulance to come."

That evening Mr. Masaba regained consciousness, but his leg was injured. It was the kind of injury that Mum was protecting us from when she ordered us to stay inside.

Where we lived was practically on the Equator. There were no seasons. The tropical weather had its own character: sunny, warm and humid the whole year round. It often rained without warning, coming down heavily for anywhere from ten minutes to an hour. Sometimes it hailed, with hailstones the size of tiny white pearls. I loved to eat them. The rain left a muddy smell. Afterward everything dried out fast.

CHAPTER 3

When I was 5 we lived near the Uganda-Congo border in a small town called Kabale. This scenic green valley town, surrounded by mountains, is heavily cultivated. This transportation hub brought daily buses filled with passengers on their way to Rwanda or Congo. When it would rain I would squat like a frog by the wheels of a newly-arrived bus. The wheels and tires would be filled with fresh mud. With my tiny fingers, I would scrape it off and eat it up. It was delicious, and when I tasted it, I felt happy.

In Entebbe in the evenings during grasshopper season, the yellow road lights attracted a lot of bright long-horned greenish grasshoppers. Natives call them Nsenene. They were a delicacy for the Africans. They would strip off the insects' wings, then fry them with onions. They said the grasshoppers tasted like shrimp and contained protein.

Our African neighbors would gather under the streetlights, then start running, jumping, shouting, and making weird sounds. As they did this, they were collecting Nsenene for their meals. Mostly women did this work.

Mum didn't like them making weird sounds. One Sunday morning Mum called to Bina, to bring the hair oil. It was oil she rubbed into our scalps—good for the eyes and brain, she said. Mum started with Donna, who wanted to go first so she could watch *Bonanza* on TV. Mum started rubbing vigorously.

"Ouch!" Donna cried. "That hurts. You're rubbing too hard Mum."

"It has to be rubbed hard," Mum told her. "The oil has to penetrate deep into your skin. It will make your hair look healthier and grow longer. This is one of the best oils. It took me a lot of time to collect different kinds of rose pedals and extract the oil from them."

As Mum was rubbing in the oil, Enoks's mum stopped by, bringing a package.

"Madam, here, this is for you" said Enko's mum. "Mimi Kuja Asante (I came to thank you)," she said in Swahili.

"For what?" Mum asked.

"Remember, last week you helped me carry some bags."

"Oh, yes. That's not a big deal," Mum said.

Mum thanked her. "Put it on that bench. Both my hands are oily."

After Enoks's mother left, Mum rubbed the oil from her hands. "I wonder what's in the package," she said to Donna. "Maybe boiled peanuts. I like them. They give them a special flavor by steaming them in banana leaves." After rubbing off the last oil, Mum opened the package. Her smile faded. "Ah, no!" she said, throwing the package away. "What in the hell are these people eating"?

Donna looked in the package and found small creatures with heads and tails. "They're cooked Nsenene, Mum. I saw people catching them last night."

Mum was a vegetarian. She would not allow any non-vegetarian food inside the house, nor would she allow anyone to use her pots to cook it. Once a week, when Papa cooked chicken, he did it in the backyard in a separate pot.

The neighborhood where we lived was mostly populated by well-educated Africans—young native couples with children.

Maria Walugembe was our next-door neighbor. Our properties shared a common wall. She lived with her husband Godfrey, and her two little boys, ages 8 and 6. Maria's 14-year-old sister Nakato, moved in with them so she could attend the Swahili primary school in Entebbe. Her village had no schools. Nakato was athletic, tall, broad-shouldered, and had short curly hair and a dry smile. Staying with them to help with cooking, cleaning and other work, was Godfrey's 10-year-old niece, Sunday. She was my height, skinny, and had a lot of curly hair. Her hair was bigger than her head. She was not intelligent, so she didn't attend school.

Godfrey was a slim, quiet person, about 5 foot 10 inches tall. He dressed smartly, and was mild-mannered. He spoke only when necessary. At 5 foot 6 inches, Maria was bright and pretty. Both of them had good jobs in offices. Maria was a secretary in the town hall and Godfrey worked in a local bank.

That was when I was 11. I was small for my age, with brown skin. I was strong, athletic, determined, and full of life. I was smart, shrewd, courageous, curious and unpredictable. I got in trouble often, and when anything went wrong, I usually took the blame. I took part in many activities, and was always ready to learn more than I could handle.

When our school was in a music competition, I tried to

learn how to play the sitar. My teacher showed me how to tune the strings for the raga: "Sa, Re, Ga Ma Pa, Dha, Ni Sa Re Ga." That's all I remember.

I loved to be stylish, and I tried to dress in modern fashions. One day, I asked Bina: "Would you trim my hair?"

"No, I won't," she said. "You know as well as I that Papa doesn't like girls to have short hair. He says it makes them look like boys."

"Please," I said. "I never ever asked you for anything. Besides, I help you with your homework all the time."

"Okay," she agreed. "I'll trim, but only a little."

Bina took the scissors, and we crawled under our parent's bed, the safest place we could think of. It was morning. Mum was in the kitchen. Papa had gone for a walk after breakfast. I lay, relaxed, my hair toward Bina. I could hear the clicking sound of the scissors as they moved from right to left.

"Here is this what you wanted?" she asked, handing me a handful of trimmed hair.

"This is nothing," I said. "Trim some more."

"Papa will get mad," she said weakly.

"He won't even notice," I said.

As I kept insisting, Bina caved in. The scissors went 'Crunch, crunch.' It was a sound I enjoyed.

"Okay, this is it," she said finally.

We both emerged, looking this way and that to make sure no one was in the bedroom. I tried to hold my hair together. I couldn't.

"This is too short," I snapped.

"You're the one who told me to keep on trimming," she retorted.

We were both scared. We knew what would happen if Papa found out. Bina pulled my hair to the back of my head and tied it with a rubber band. We both knew this wouldn't hold my hair for long. For the next three days I kept it in a ponytail, and tried to keep from facing Papa. Then, on the third day, he saw.

"What happened to your hair?" he shouted.

Seeing the anger in Papa's eyes, Bina ran away.

"Who cut your hair?" Papa demanded.

"Bina," I confessed. "I told her to trim it, and she cut it too short."

We both got punished.

But from then on I kept my hair short all the time. The two boring hair plaits hanging on both sides of my ears were gone forever. I loved my new hairstyle. Every weekend, I rolled my hair up in curlers. My curls came out nicely and swung from right to left as I moved. I felt like a diva. After a while, I walked slowly on my toes. I also had bangs falling towards one side, covering my forehead.

I felt that my new look was flattering, and for the first time I didn't mind Mum washing my hair. I'd always felt suffocated when Mum pushed my soapy long hair over my face. Sometimes it made me cry. Her only response was to tell me to keep quiet. When it was washed, she then rubbed in the oil. I hated having greasy hair, but she gave me no choice.

From time to time I upset Sunday with my playfulness. Every evening before dusk it was her job to make sure all the cocks, chickens, and chicks were in their coop. It was fun watching her chase them. They ran as fast as they could, always clucking.

One day a thought crossed my mind. "Bina," I whispered, "let's hide some of the chicks."

"No." She refused.

I looked at her. "If you won't help, I'll do it on my own." Picking up two chicks, I wrapped them in my dress. I hid them in a deep bucket, then sat on it, waiting to see Sunday's reaction. As she got the chicks into the coop, she counted: "Moja, mbili, tatu, nne, tano, sita, saba…" She stopped. Her fingers disappeared into her big hood of hair as she scratched her scalp. She re-counted. "There are supposed to be nine. I have only seven." She started looking everywhere. "Ambapo ni mapumziko ya vifaranga wangu?" she screamed. "Where are the rest of my chicks?" Her eyes filled with tears. "My aunty is going to punish me." It was true. Sunday's Aunt Maria was strict about losing things.

I tried to keep a straight face, but it was hard. Finally I smiled knowingly.

"You're hiding my chicks," she snapped.

"No," I replied, holding my smile.

"Give her chicks back to her," Bina whispered.

"Let her cry a little more," I said.

Sunday, picked up a stick and ran after me. She stopped when she heard her Uncle Godfrey's scooter.

I laughed. "You see? You can't catch me." Finally I turned over the bucket so they could run out. "Here are your chicks," I said. "Go catch them."

"I won't speak to you again," she said angrily. She turned and left.

That evening I began to feel sorry for giving Sunday a hard time.

I was also good at hiding myself. When we played

hide-and-seek, I would crawl under bushes, or lie down in wild grass. I enjoyed fooling the others.

We lived in a rental house in a small valley. It was within walking distance of the main church, and had a view of the north end of Lake Victoria. In this small valley, there were more than sixty duplex houses, all seemingly built as a single project. They stood in two rows facing each other, and were separated by a narrow gutter and a road. It was a safe, peaceful, friendly neighborhood. Every house had a front yard, side yard and back yard. The back yard was mostly for gardens, while some had chicken and turkey stalls. Fruit trees, including mango, coconut, avocado, plantain and banana, stood in the yards of almost every house. Cassavas were planted at the very end of the garden. They multiplied rapidly, forming a fence. Our garden had no cassava plants. Mum thought they created a hiding place for intruders.

At our house Mum had her vegetable and flower gardens. The dwarf coconut tree at the corner of the house was about my height. Its five big branches spread in each direction, and it held a nest of mini-coconuts, each the size of a walnut, in its center. The banana tree, close to the back door, didn't produce much: hardly one banana loop yearly.

The toilet was out in the backyard, a few meters away, and between both houses. The walkway from backdoor to toilet was straight. Behind the toilet was a huge wild government property. We called it "no man's land." It had its own natural beauty, with golden bamboo trees and a few fruit trees. The only time we went there was to pick fruits, especially the jackfruit, whose tree was close to

our vegetable garden. The giant jackfruit tree had a lot of fruits which shook the ground when they fell, as if there'd been an earthquake.

One thing we loved, but didn't grow in our garden, was the cassava root. We had friends who gave these to us whenever we wanted them. The cassava (or "mogo" in Swahili) is yummy when fried, and sprinkled with salt and chili, or cooked in tomato sauce with cumin seeds. In school every day at recess, we all bought small plates of cooked cassava for less than a shilling each. Cooked Indian style, with tomatoes and green chilis, it was delicious. Two Indian ladies made it, then carried the big pot all the way from their house to school to make extra money. For the natives the cassava is an important staple, often pounded into flour. The cassava flour is steamed and served with vegetables for lunch.

Our house was small, and with seven people, we had to share beds. The two-story bed was set in the corner of the living room. I shared the bottom with Donna, while Bina shared the top with Kevin. Jaimini slept in the master bedroom.

We loved sleeping in the living room. We watched our favorite TV programs while lying in bed. I always covered my head to keep from seeing anything scary in shows like *Lost In Space*, *Time Tunnel* and *Star Trek*.

Life was good.

The two dwarf bushy trees in the backyard made a good place to sit, or, where they came together to make a hollow space beneath, it was the perfect hiding place. We would cover it with a bed sheet, making it into a secret house where we could hide from our friends.

I was especially concerned with keeping this spot hidden from Daksha Shah. Daksha was my classmate. Whenever she came to play, she stole one of my toy kitchen utensils. Once, when I noticed my rolling pin was missing, I saw it sitting at her house.

"This is mine," I said. "Look, the color is peeled off at the corner."

Snatching it from my hand, she put it, and all her own utensils, away. I ran home sobbing. Mum said we shouldn't play with her anymore.

From that day on, whenever we saw Daksha coming down the hill, we hid ourselves in our secret space. Mum would tell Daksha we were not home, but Daksha didn't believe her. The girl walked through our house, searching, but soon she got tired of it. Feeling miserable, she would finally leave.

CHAPTER 4

My siblings and I were very close, and didn't need any other playmates. On Sundays and during vacations,, we played near the lakeshore or at the National Botanical Gardens, both of which were within easy walking distance.

The Botanical Gardens were our favorite. Besides being educational, it was a chance to pick exotic fruits. On the way to the botanical gardens we passed neighbors' houses, then farmland. Natives grew potatoes and sweet potatoes on the farmland, and there were a few mango trees. Most were too high for us to reach. We picked up the ones that had fallen on the ground. They were brownish to greenish when unripe and changed to reddish, yellowish when ripe. Good for making mango pulp. A dirt path went between the gardens and the grasslands. Either way we would see some of the most breathtaking scenery one could imagine.

The Botanical Gardens were a weekend getaway for many. Every weekend they were packed with locals and with tourists from all over Uganda, especially from Kampala. It was a perfect place for a picnic.

Most of the huge trees were one, two, or even three centuries old. Their buttress roots made a perfect spot for us to play. We played the Mum-and-Dad game, naming the spaces between the roots: our bedroom, our kitchen and our playroom.

The gardens were 40 hilly hectares (over 80 acres) set near Lake Victoria's shores. It was fun to slide down the hill sitting on a sheet of cardboard. The keepers divided the plants by region (temperate, tropical, etc.), and by theme (rock garden, medicinal garden, etc.). The rain forest had wild life, including black and white colobus monkeys, and birds such as the hornbill. Everywhere there were exotic plants.

Many of the trees were so tall that we would hurt our necks trying to see their tops. The Tarzan creepers hanging down from the trees were good enough for us to hold and swing on, but we couldn't compete with the colobus monkeys. They would watch our lame efforts, then start performing downward leaps of fifteen or twenty feet. Using their long shoulder hair to form parachutes, they would grasp the vines and swing from one vine to another, making creaking and rattling sounds. If we brought food near them, these monkeys would snatch it. The monkeys never left the forest. It was too cool and comfortable.

One had to be careful walking this path. Some of the tropical plants had razor-like leaves that could cut a person's skin. One could hear the sound of the water dripping down the taro leaves one after another, till it reached Mother Earth.

Then there was a waterfall, whose fresh pure water ran down the mountain. The frequent rainfalls provided local residents with crystal clear drinking water all the year round. Most of the rural areas had no running water, so native women carried it on their heads in square tin containers called "duba." They could lift about seventy percent of their body weight and carry it about 15 kilometers to their huts. Some made this trip back and forth two or three times a day. Many had their babies strapped to their backs the whole time.

Around these waterfalls, exotic butterflies, big and small, flew everywhere. These butterflies seemed accustomed to people. They flew close and didn't try to avoid us. A boy I knew named Jack gathered cocoons and caterpillars in a glass bottle. He'd made small holes on the lid to give them air.

"It's for my class," he said, putting some in his pocket.

"But they'll die," I protested.

"It's for my dinner," he said.

But his mother said, "I'm tired of this boy. He won't listen to anyone and he does mischievous things."

Immigrants from the world-over brought exotic fruits and trees to the gardens, such as elephant apples, jambula, the sausage tree, and the coco tree. The rubber tree was amazing to watch. Rubber drops from the tree looked like tears running down.

Near the rubber tree was a boxing tree, with soft fibrous bark that we could punch with our fists. One Saturday, when we were there with a bunch of other children, our self-appointed leader, Joshna, said: "Boys all of you, stand on that side. Girls stand on this side. We'll have a competition. The one who boxes hardest wins a prize."

We girls were anxious to win. The boxing went on for hours. Finally the mischievous Jack pushed everyone out of the way, and knocked hard with his wrist.

"You won," said Joshna, handing him a star fruit. "Here's your prize."

"What kind of a prize is this?" Jack said, angrily tossing the fruit as far as he could. We all laughed.

"Jack, could you and your friends climb the jambula tree for us?" Meenakshi asked.

"Is it already jambula season?" he asked.

"Yes, it's May. We have two full months to enjoy these fruits." Meenakshi finished by telling us to be there the following Saturday.

Though Jack was naughty, he'd also been the only boy who insisted that his friends help us girls get jambula fruit.

The next Saturday we arrived on time, but Jack was nowhere to be seen.

"He won't come back," said one of the girls, but a half hour later he appeared.

"Look, there he is," said Bina.

We saw Jack bribing the Askari (watchman) with a pack of cigarettes. The Askari was our nemesis in the gardens, always chasing us off whenever we tried to get any fruit from the trees. Without his cooperation we couldn't actually pick any fruit. The cigarettes bought that cooperation.

With the Askari turning a blind eye, the boys climbed the tree, and jambula fruit showered onto the ground. We ate what we could of the sweet, astringent fruit while filling our bags.

"Look," I said, pointing to Lata's mouth. "Your tongue is purple."

"Yours too," said Lata. "Make sure you don't get it on your clothes. It won't go away with the wash."

"Will you be here next Saturday, Jack?" Bina asked.

"No," said the mischievous, but useful boy.

"Why not?"

"I have to help my father in his shop," he replied. Jack's father owned a shoe repair shop on the elite shopping street. He was well known for the quality leather shoes he sold,

So the following week we were on our own. None of us had any cigarettes for the Askari, so we had to be careful.

Joshna said, "Mila, you stand and watch for the Askari. Bina and Lata will climb the tree Meenakshi you pick the fallen fruits".

I stood guard as Lata and Bina started climbing. Though clumps of fruit hung from the lower branches, their task wasn't easy. They made it to the first branch and shook it.

That's when we heard the Askari. "You!" he sputtered, hurrying toward us. "You are back again. How many times have I told you; picking fruits from this garden is prohibited." He threw his stick at us.

I and some others ran and hid behind a tree. Lata and Bina jumped down, but Bina fell, hurting her knees and arm. She scrambled to her feet, and they both ran. We hid behind one of the trees.

The Askari, a tall man who carried a big stick and a whistle draped around his neck stood under the jambula tree for a while in his khaki shorts and shirt, looking this way and that.

"Don't laugh, Mila," Joshna whispered.

Finally he left.

"He's gone," said Lata, and we all emerged from our hiding places.

I started cracking up, and the rest were infected with my laughter.

"We'll have to tell Jack about this," Meenakshi said. "Let's pick some more before the Askari comes back."

The jambula fruit is oval shaped, and looks like a very large berry. As it matures it goes from pink to shining crimson black. It tastes like a cherry, and leaves a reddish purple stain on the tongue, or on one's clothing. Mum would be angry if we came home with dark stains on our dresses. She'd told us not to pick those fruits.

The cinnamon trees and black pepper trees were in the medicinal zone of the gardens. The cinnamon tree looked normal to passersby, but we knew we could break off bits of the inner bark and put them into our pockets for later. It had a spicy flavor.

CHAPTER 5

During summer vacations we helped with the house chores and played.

One June day Bina put on her new checked slacks, and I could see that she was going out.

"Where are you going?" I asked.

"Joshna's house," Bina replied.

"Can I come too?" I asked.

"No," she said abruptly.

Earlier I'd heard Joshna and Meenakshi whispering, and I figured it out. They were going to the lake shore to pick coco. I wanted to pick coco too. "Mum!" I cried.

"What is it?" Mum asked.

"They're going to lake shore to pick coco, but they won't take me."

Mum said to Bina. "You are not stepping out of the house without Mila."

I smiled. They hadn't known I was listening, but now they had to let me come along.

When we got there, Meenakshi wasn't happy to see me. A year older than Bina, Meenakshi was a cunning manipulator who liked to gossip about boys. She made a face at me, and told me to stay behind the rest of them. "You can follow us," she said.

Meenakshi, Bina and Joshna walked together, while I followed them across the farmland into the wilderness. Once we were past the fields, we took the narrow path through the grasslands. It was bordered by swampy wetlands, and we had to be careful not to fall into the muddy water. We went single-file.

From there the shore looked glorious, as extravagant blooms of fascia mingled with the grasslands. Colorful butterflies hovered, spreading their wings over the wildflowers. Meenakshi, Joshna and I stopped, and tried to catch the butterflies. We knelt quietly on the grass, which was about half my height. We watched the butterflies pull the juice out of the flowers, then picked them up by their wings. We looked at them, and released them. It was fun.

Bina didn't stop with the rest of us. Instead she walked towards the shore. She lost herself in the waves, splashing her feet. The tide was coming in. As the tide got higher, she pulled herself away and looked up.

"What's that?" she wondered, as the edge of a big dark cloud came into view above the cliff. "It's moving this way." She raised her voice, pointing, "Mila, Meenakshi, Joshna, come look."

I stood and glanced up. "It's just a cloud," I said, sitting back down. Bina kept shouting. I stood up. "Why are you shouting so loud?"

She pointed. "Look. It's moving towards us."

The three of us ran closer to the shore and saw what she meant. "Wow!" I said. "What could that be? Clouds don't move this fast."

"You didn't want to believe me," said Bina. I shaded my eyes with my hand, and focused. "It's a school of mosquitoes headed right for us. Run!"

As we ran, Meenakshi fell down, screaming, "They're all over me. Help me. Someone please, help me."

We stopped and looked around, but couldn't see her. "Where are you?" Bina called.

Finally we saw Meenakshi lying in the grasses. "Meenakshi," Bina called. "We're over here. Get up and run."

Hearing Bina's voice, Meenakshi stood up.

"There she is!" Joshna cried.

Meenakshi's eyes and face were all swollen from mosquito bites, and it took her a moment to focus.

"You're on the wrong path," shouted Bina. "We're over here."

Finally Meenakshi turned and followed us. Soon we

reached the garden entrance. There we were careful to avoid the streaming columns of dangerous ants.

We were out of breath and thirsty. We walked towards the waterfall and sat down on a big stone near the stream. The mosquito bites were all over our faces, legs, and hands. Meenakshi's bites were the worst.

"I'm not feeling good," she said. "My whole body is itching and burning."

"Don't scratch," said Bina. "It will only make it worse. Look, you're making red spots on your body. Take this mud and put on there." The cool mud helped ease Meenakshi's itching. Bina helped her rub it on her legs, arms, neck and face, making Meenakshi look like an alien.

Bina turned on me, and shouted, "It's your fault. Whenever you are with us, something happens. We didn't even get a chance to pick the coco."

"Oh, yeah," I countered.

"You're the one who stood at the shore instead of walking towards the coco plants," she argued. "You were too busy picking up butterflies, and you talked Meenakshi and Joshna into staying there with you."

"Stop your nonsense, both of you," Joshna screamed.

Bina and I fell silent.

Instead of continuing our fight, we all sat for hours watching the monkeys swinging from one branch to another in-between the branches of the huge tree, one could see the sun move gently away to make space for the dark blue clouds. Finally it started to get dark. We were there, alone, and night would soon be falling. All at once it became very quiet. The only sounds to be heard was the leaves on the trees whispering with each other and frogs crocking. The monkeys moved slowly to find a place between the branches to spend their night safely.

"Let's go home," said Meenakshi. A tall, fair-skinned girl, she had a weak constitution. She was vulnerable, and seemed like she was easily influenced, but she was not. She looked to her right and left, shaking from fear and cold she held her hands tightly.

As we walked home Bina warned me. "Don't you tell Mum what happened. She would never allow us to go to the shore anymore."

"Only if you apologize," I demanded. At first Bina refused, but when the other girls got after her, she apologized. As I heard her apology I felt proud. Finally we all decided to keep this our secret.

We walked quickly towards Joshna's house. In the falling darkness we didn't realize that a lost baby monkey was following us. When we reached Joshna's house, we washed the mud off and rubbed a cooling cream on our skin. Then we got up to go home.

As Joshna opened the front door to let us out, the monkey leapt out from behind the flowerpot, ready to jump on us. We got back inside the door, and locked it.

"Where did this monkey come from?" I asked.

"If we try to walk home it will bite us," Bina said. "Haven't we already gotten enough bites from all those mosquitoes?"

"You can stay here overnight if you want to," said Joshna. "Meenakshi is going to stay. We can all play Antakshari* before bedtime."

---

*Each contestant sings two complete lines of Hindi movie songs that begins with the Hindustani consonant on which the previous contestant's song selection ended.

"Oh, no," I said. "If we won't show up on time, our mum will never allow us to go play anymore."

We watched the front door, which was the only exit, and waited another twenty minutes. We peered out from a small window. The monkey was nowhere to be seen.

"I think the monkey's gone," Joshna said, opening the front door. As we stepped outside the monkey leapt out from behind the flowerpot. It tipped over the pot, and practically flew past Joshna into the house at full speed. Bina and I ran.

Finally we were on our way home. As we walked, Bina told me, "I'd seen this monkey following us from the forest, but I ignored it because of the itching."

The following Saturday, when I visited Joshna, she was squeezing dark purple passion fruits for juice. She added a little salt and offered me a drink. It was refreshing.

"Hey look, Joshna," I said. "The guava tree is loaded with fruit. Can I pick some?"

"Go ahead," she said.

I took a bucket and climbed the tree. As I stretched my arm towards one of the branches, big round eyes stared at me. I stood still. "Why is this monkey still in Joshna's backyard?" I asked myself. I let the bucket fall and climbed down. At the bottom I tripped over a branch, but quickly got up and ran towards the kitchen. "There's a monkey!" I screamed.

The monkey closed in on me as I tried to climb the stairs to the kitchen. It grasped my dress in its mouth and got a piece of my skirt. "Help!" I screamed.

Joshna came out and threw a rolling pin at it, but the monkey wasn't scared at all. It ran towards Joshna, who retreated into the kitchen and locked the door. With the monkey focused on her, I had a chance to run to the back gate. I threw the wooden door open, and got behind it, where the monkey wouldn't notice me. This little round-eyed animal saw the open gate and ran out of the yard. I slammed the gate behind me. I had some scratches on my arms and legs, but I was okay. I'd lost a piece from my new dress, and one of my golden earrings, but otherwise everything was all right.

I later learned that Joshna, an animal lover, had been feeding and nurturing this baby monkey all week.

CHAPTER 6

A couple of miles from the Botanical Gardens was a
zoo. It had tigers, lions, giraffes, elephants, monkeys,
snakes, rhinos, crocodiles and more. I only went to the
zoo during guava and passion fruit season. At the short
fence at the entrance there were many of these fruits
ready to pick.

One Saturday afternoon, as we walked through the
farmland towards the Botanical Gardens, an African boy
jumped out from behind the bushes. He grasped my
right wrist.

"Run," Meenakshi shouted, and everyone ran away. I
looked around and saw I was alone with this boy.

"Please let me go," I pleaded.

"Don't twist your hands," he said, tightening his grip
on me.

"Ouch! That hurts."

He laughed, made big eyes at me, and said: "I want to
marry you."

I got scared, and wanted to cry. I knew I must escape,
but how? I kicked him hard but he was stronger than
me. "Help!" I screamed. The more I screamed the more
this boy liked it.

"I want to marry you," he repeated again and again.

Then I had an idea. "I accept your offer," I said, "but I need to go home to get my best clothes so I can look pretty during the wedding."

"No," he said. "If I let you go, you will not come back."

I smiled and told him: "Don't worry. I will definitely come back." Somehow this convinced him.

He let my hand loose, and said: "Okay. Go bring your things. I will wait for you here."

I ran and ran as fast as my legs could take me. I didn't look back. When I got to my house, I went straight into the living room. I peered out of the window, but didn't see him.

Bina and her friends were sitting there playing card games.

"Why did you leave me all alone with that boy?" I demanded.

"We were afraid," Bina said. I cried and kicked their cards, scattering them.

The next day I was too scared to leave the house.

"Why don't you go play outside?" asked Donna.

"I'm not feeling good," I said.

"You're lying," she said. She saw my pale face.

For the next two weeks I did not dare go to the fields.

Finally a Sunday morning came when I very much wanted to play outside, but I was still afraid that the boy might be nearby.

Noticing my discomfort, Papa asked: "What's the matter?"

"Nothing."

"Then why are you upset?"

I didn't answer.

"Every weekend you get your sisters and brother to go to the lake or to the Botanical Gardens, but today you are as quiet as a mouse. There is something you are not telling me."

Now the words came out of me. "The last time we were out, an African boy came out of nowhere and grabbed my hand tight. I screamed, but Bina and her friends left me behind with him. I kept screaming, but no one came. I finally escaped, but I'm still afraid."

"Bina," Papa called angrily. "Mila has told me what happened with that African boy. Why did you run away? Four of you can't beat up one little boy? What if this boy did something to harm your sister?"

Bina looked down and said: "We got scared."

"Anyway, I am glad you are safe," said Papa.

After that he told Mum. They decided we would all go to the main beach after lunch. We had an early lunch at eleven am. While we did the dishes, Mum put on a colorful sari with a matching blouse (Sari is a long piece of clothing worn from hips to the ankle over the under frock with a blouse covering the chest),and Papa took a short nap, then around two o'clock we headed for the lake.

Papa loved long walks. That was okay with Mum as long as the whole family was going. The beach we were going to was close to the airport. Like the Botanical gardens, tourists flocked there on the weekends. On our way we stopped at our favorite playground. From there, we could see the blue-grayish lake.

The breeze was cool and full of the refreshing scent of the water. This energized us.

There was a cannon that was a war memorial. We called it "the Top." We broke away from our parents and ran toward it, wanting to climb it. We climbed around the cannon for a while, then Mum and Papa said it was time to get to the beach.

At the beach Mum found a place to spread two makekos (beach mats) on the sand. Papa lay down.

"Watch Jaimini," Mum told Papa. Mum took off her sari, leaving her under frock and blouse, and went in the water. It was weird to watch the Indian ladies swimming in their long under frock and a sari blouse. Mum knew how to swim on her back.

Bina and I took off our dresses, leaving our petticoats on. The water was nice and warm. We played with the waves and threw water on each other.

Bina said, "I'm going to walk further and see how deep this lake is."

"It's too deep," I told her. "You'll drown."

"I won't go too far," she said. "I'll only let the water come up to my chest."

I stood watching as Bina kept on paddling her feet.

"You're going too far," I shouted.

"No I am not."

I watched her go deeper and deeper until I could no longer see her chest. Suddenly her legs got caught.

"Mum! Help!" she screamed. "My legs are stuck."

She was stuck in the mud at the bottom. The big waves were rising to her neck. Mum was swimming with the other ladies far from us. There were a lot of people. She couldn't hear.

"Help," I shouted. "Someone please help my sister. She's drowning."

An 18-year-old athletic boy named Harish heard me screaming.

"Over there!" I pointed.

He jumped into the water and rescued Bina. Mother came from the water to see what was going on. Everyone was watching.

"You were not supposed to go out that far," Mum shouted.

"I won't do it again," Bina wept.

Mum dried herself and put on her sari. She gave us snacks and drinks.

Kevin and Donna were building a castle, and Kevin enlisted my help. We soaked sand with water, and started building the walls. Kevin and I dug around the castle, making a moat. Then I noticed Kevin scratching down into the sand in a single place.

"What are you doing?" I asked.

"There's something stuck here," he said. "I'm trying to pull it out." Suddenly he got it. "Look what I found. It's a bottle of Coke. Wow!"

This was a great find. Our parents never bought us soft drinks. We sat and stared at the bottle. Papa opened it with his teeth and handed it over to Kevin. Kevin took a sip and passed it to us. It was cold, fizzy, sugary and delicious. We felt blessed.

Further down the beach a few African boys aged between 8 and 12 were diving from the top of the cliff. They looked like they were having a lot of fun.

As the daylight waned, the orange-red sun reflected on the waters.

"Oh my God," I said, seeing the watch on Papa's hand. "It's already 6 o'clock. Come! Hurry up! We need to go home! *Batman* starts at 7. We can't miss that. It's a continuation from last week."

"Then hurry up," Mum said. Mum took Jaimini and Kevin to the water to clean the sand off. Meanwhile Papa shook the Makeko and rolled it up.

Mum handed a plastic bag to Bina. "Here fill this with sand." It was soft white powdery sand that was good for scrubbing pots and pans. "Mila, you carry the bag of snacks."

On our way, Papa carried Kevin on his shoulders while Mum carried Jaimini. Bina took the house keys. She, Donna and I jogged ahead, hoping to reach home in time.

Papa felt grateful for the day. He'd had a full rest and enjoyed the fresh breeze. We were living in this beautiful town where we had everything we needed.

CHAPTER 7

The main road from Kampala to Entebbe went to the airport. Along some stretches there were two shopping streets with businesses owned by Guajarati's, and a few owned by Muslim's. The one closest to the airport was on higher ground than the other. We called that the elite, white people's shopping street. It had very few stores, but was surrounded by residences. In the commercial part there were retail stores, and across from them stood a bank and a few office buildings.

The shopping street down the hill had many retail stores, and at the very end, a butcher shop owned by a native. As in many parts of East Africa, there were three communities: a white upper class, an Indian middle class, and the native Ugandan Africans, or nationals. Each group lived in its own neighborhood. The white folks lived closer to the airport, and had their own private beaches, while the Indians and the Muslims lived in the town. A very few, including my family, lived in the neighborhood of educated Africans on the outskirts of town. The rest of the native tribes, mostly uneducated, lived on the plantations or up in the hills.

Most of Entebbe's housing was for the civil servants working in the government ministries. Others residents made their livings from agriculture. In this small town few people owned cars. Some rode bicycles or scooters, but the majority walked.

One of the biggest coffee plantations was managed by Rameshbhai Patel, father of a girl named Neelu, who was Bina's classmate. The plantation was located behind the police station in the northeast, on the little elevation between the two shopping centers. The only way to reach it was by a narrow dirt road. There was also a manmade path between the coffee plants. It was a shortcut, but not an easy one. During coffee season the branches bent low across the path, forcing travelers to push them out of the way. Also this shorter path was isolated, making it more dangerous. My sisters and I preferred the short cut.

Mum did the sewing work for Neelu's family. I was the one who had to go back and forth, either to drop off or pick up the clothing. After breakfast on our first day of vacation, Mum handed me a bag full of dresses and blouses which she had just finished sewing.

"Drop these at Neelu's house," she said. "While you're there, get the shillings from them."

It was hot, and I didn't want to do it. "I have to catch up on my homework," I said. "Papa wants me to finish it by noon." This was a rule in our house: on Saturday morning after breakfast we had to study at least one hour before helping Mum with the cooking.

"Don't worry," Mum said. "I will let your Papa know you are going to the farm."

That made me angry. "Why me?" I demanded. "Why can't Bina go?"

Mum raised her voice: "Start going."

I went. As I walked along I muttered to myself, wondering why I was the one who got trapped into this.

Neelu lived with her parents, brother, sister-in-law and their two adorable children. Their big wooden house sat on a small hill in the middle of the plantations. It took less than an hour to walk there. As I passed by the shops, I thought of stopping at Mr. Raja's to see if his daughter, Lena, one of my school friends, would go with me. Mr. Raja owned one of my favorite stores where I could always get a free ice stick. I would say: "Mr. Raja, it's very hot today. Can I have one ice stick?" He always handed me one, saying: "Here you are, but don't come back again." I always thanked him and walked away feeling happy.

I waited at the corner until the big line of customers was gone, then I stood at the counter, looking at him. Mr. Raja was a tall, skinny, round-faced, fair-skinned man.

"Are you here for an ice stick?" he asked looking down at me.

"No, I came to ask if Lena can walk with me to the coffee farm."

"Lena is not at home," he said. "She's gone to her auntie's house in Lira. She left yesterday evening." He opened the refrigerator, and pulled out an ice stick. "Here," he said, smiling. "I know you won't go unless I give you one."

I happily walked away licking the ice stick. As I neared the police station my head was getting hot. I pulled a big napkin from my pocket, wet it with my drinking water, and covered my head.

A big crowd had gathered outside the police station. Curious, I squeezed through the crowd. There was a goat chained to a tree.

"Why is this goat chained?" I asked one of the men.

"They took this goat out of a python's mouth," he said.

"That's awful," I said, and I walked away. I picked up a stick to fend off any snakes I might encounter. Neelu's sister-in-law welcomed me. I handed over the bag of clothing.

"Sit here," she said. "I will be right back." She took the clothing and went into her bedroom. I waited and waited. A cool breeze from the fan blew over my body. I felt drowsy. I heard a door opening, then footsteps. I became alert.

"Mila, your mum is a good seamstress," said Neelu's sister-in-law. "She did a great job. All the blouses fitted perfectly. Here." She handed me the shillings. "Put them in your bag."

Just then Neelu's mother walked in. "Hello, Mila. Did you bring the clothing?"

"Yes, Aunty," I said.

"Good. Go play with Neelu while I make lunch. You will stay for lunch, won't you?"

I said I would, and went out looking for Neelu. I called her name, and found her in the stream, walking on the coffee beans as she washed them.

"Mila," she called. "I'm over here, come. Come on. It's fun."

I took off my slippers. She took my hand and pulled me. The water was nice and cool. "Wow!" I said.

We rolled our feet on the beans. The water was pushing them into a huge strainer. I'd seen Neelu's father as he'd supervised workers who put tons of coffee beans into the stream, and I had fun watching them.

Now Neelu's father pointed. "Look, at the end of the stream. All these coffee beans will be separated from the bad ones in that strainer. They will then fill big bags. Once they're bagged we take them to have them roasted."

Some coffee beans looked like big cherries. I couldn't resist the temptation to eat them. Neelu and I threw coffee beans on each other. Then all three of us returned to the house for lunch.

After lunch Neelu's mum gave me some roasted coffee beans. I carefully filled my pocket with them, saving them for later.

"Aunty, thank you for the lunch," I said. "Now I have to go back home."

"I wish you could stay a little longer," said Neelu.

"I would love to," I replied, "but my mum will be waiting for me." I took my bag and walked out.

"Wait," said Neelu's father. "I will take you home. I have to go to town to drop these bags."

"It is no longer safe to walk all by yourself, Mila. Two of my employees went missing yesterday." he said. I could see Neelu's father holding back his tears.

One of his employees sat at the back. He carried a tool to protect us.

"Thank you," I said, glad that I didn't have to walk.

I had to wait until Neelu's father had taken his after-lunch nap. Neelu and I chatted on the balcony until he woke up at about three. After having his afternoon tea, he pulled a small truck in front of the house and commanded his workers to load the back with bags. The bags appeared to be too heavy, and I asked: "Are those coffee beans?"

"Yes, they are," said Neelu's father. He opened the front door. "Get in."

I felt proud to sit in the front seat of his truck.

On arriving home I cried out, "Mum, where are you?"

"I'm in the backyard," she called. As I went out there, Mum said, "Why are you so late?"

"I stayed for lunch. Neelu's father told me that two of his employees disappeared and that it is not safe for me to walk by myself. Mum, he was upset." I said.

Mum, busy with her work, responded, "Oh yeah?" and carried on.

"It's a lot of work taking all the heavy mattresses out into the lawn. Did the blouses fit well?"

"Yes, Mum. Her sister-in law said to thank you and she said you are a very good sewer. Here are the shillings."

Mum stuck the shilling notes in the side of her sari blouse. "Help me open the side of these mattresses," she said. She did this once a year to ventilate the cotton and kill any bugs. I would soon enjoy the soft warmth of the cotton, as I sank into the mattress.

CHAPTER 8

In the early evening, after a long day, Mum sat on the backdoor steps, thinking, *I'm tired. What shall I cook for dinner?* She glanced at her vegetable garden and the fruit trees to see if anything caught her eye. At that moment a huge jackfruit fell from the tree with a thud. "There you go," she said to herself. "This will be a good and easy dinner. But how am I going to pick up this giant jackfruit? It's too heavy." She looked around to see if there was anyone who could help her. "Sunday," Mum called. She got no answer. "Sunday, where are you?"

Sunday, our next-door girl, was lying in the hallway. She was a lazy one. She only worked when commanded by her aunty. The rest of the time she would either sit or sleep.

When Mum called a third time, Sunday wandered out, rubbing her eyes.

"Mrs. Saita, what is it?" she asked in Swahili.

"Could you to help me pick up that jackfruit?" Mum asked, pointing at the fruit under the tree.

"Okay," Sunday grudgingly agreed. "Let me first go to the rest room. I will be ready in a few minutes."

They both climbed the bent fence onto the government property.

As they tried to lift the jackfruit, Sunday shouted, "Oh my God, moja hii ni nzito sana." She was saying it was very heavy.

"Yes," Mum replied. "It must be thirty-five pounds or more. With all that weight, and the thorny skin, I can't carry it myself. That's why I needed your help." They threw it over the fence and climbed back into the garden. They managed to lift it onto the brick wall."

"Ow!" Sunday cried out.

"What?" Mum asked.

"My hand is bleeding." She and Mum looked at Sunday's right hand. She'd cut it on the thorny skin of the fruit.

"Go wash your hands," said Mum. "I will divide the fruit."

Mum got a knife from the kitchen, took it outside, and chopped the fruit in half. It was not easy because the knife was too short. Once she'd made the cut, she smashed the fruit on a stone, spitting it in two. As she chopped it into smaller pieces, she ate bits of the fruit.

"This one has big pieces and is very sweet," she said as Sunday returned. "You can tell from its color, nice orange and yellowish. Here, take this one, Sunday." Mum was always particular and precise in her work. She had oil and warm water ready to rub on her hands to keep the fibrous flesh from sticking.

That evening for dinner, we had the jackfruit and plantains from our African neighbors. The African folk use only the green unripe plantain for cooking. They throw away the ripe ones. Though ripe plantains are less sugary than bananas, we still liked them. They were available year-round. Plantains had a neutral taste like boiled potatoes. Mum fried them, sprinkled them with salt and red chili. They were delicious.

That evening I ate two big plantains and many pieces of the sweet jackfruit. I ate and ate, not realizing how full I was getting. My stomach felt like it would burst. Even though we all ate a lot, there were plenty of leftovers.

"Make sure you clean your hands thoroughly with oil, salt and hot water before you come in the house," Mum told us.

It had gotten too dark to go throw the leftovers into the wild growth, which we called "wilderness." We would do that in the morning. We didn't have garbage pickups back then. Instead we threw fruit skins, and other garbage into the wilderness. We recycled all newspapers and paper bags, using them to wrap and pack things until they were no longer usable. Finally they too would go to the wilderness. Mother Earth takes all, and makes it into fertilizer.

That evening I was not yet ready to go inside. I sat in the doorway watching screeching birds as they flew in "V" formations towards their nest. I wondered, why do they fly in formation?

It was dusk. "Crick, crick, crick," went the crickets. The mosquitoes came out, and flew toward the light.

"Mila," Mum called from the kitchen. "Get in the house and lock the door."

Mum went to her bedroom. After giving Jamini her bottle of milk, she finished the rest of her sewing. Papa lay in bed listening to the radio. I took out my small drums. My sisters and brother gathered around me. They sang as I played the drums. Over time we learned to chant some of the Satang songs. We sometimes did this when our parents went out for the evening.

Kevin sat crossed-legged next to Bina.

"Stop pushing on my knees," she complained.

"Someone is in the garden," he whispered.

"I can't hear you," she said. "Say it louder."

"Someone is in the garden" he repeated. "Listen!"

We all fell silent. Sounds came from outdoors. "It's only the crickets," I said. "Kevin, you're just being mischievous." I went back to drumming.

"Listen," Kevin insisted. "I'm telling the truth. I heard the sound again."

Bina went close to the door and listened. "Yes," she whispered. "I hear 'che, che, che'."

Donna ran in to Mum.

"What is it?" Mum asked.

Donna was panting with excitement and fear.

"Why are you huffing? Speak up," Mum said.

Donna pointed outside. "Someone's in the garden."

Papa turned down the radio and stood up. "I'll go check." He put his hands on Donnas' head, and said: "Don't be afraid." He took the torch flashlight and a stick he kept by the door.

He went out and aimed the light everywhere. "Hey you: Toka! Toka!" he shouted, telling whoever it was to go away. White eyes and white teeth stood out against the darkness, staring at him. Papa threw the stick at the trespasser. Our next door neighbor, Maria and Godfrey, heard papa, and looked out the window.

"What is it, Babu?" asked his wife, Maria.

"There's someone in the garden," he replied. Godfrey and Maria came out in their nightclothes. The intruder, a young man shouldering a jute bag, ran, leaving a shovel behind. Papa ran after him. The man threw the bag over the fence, pulled up both his long legs, and rolled over the top to the other side. He disappeared into the wilderness.

"What was he doing?" asked Godfrey. "Look, he dug a hole. I think he had something in that Jute bag he wanted to bury."

"But why in our garden?" Papa asked. Papa picked up the stick and found a blood-stained shirt. With his stick, he propelled it over the fence. Maria screamed and ran into her house. Papa flashed the torch behind the toilet and into to the wilderness. The man was nowhere to be seen. "He won't come here anymore," said Papa.

In the house Kevin asked: "Who was it, Papa?"

"Someone who was not supposed to be in our garden," Papa replied. "When he saw me, he fled." Papa proudly pulled up his shoulders. He set the torch and stick behind the door, and went into his room.

"Our garden can be very dangerous," Mum said to Papa.

That night, I had a stomachache. My intestines were rumbling and turning, and I felt like I had to go to the toilet. I imagined the digger was hiding somewhere in the garden that reminded me of Neelu's father's two employees disappearance, which left me too scared to go out. I held my stomach tightly, hoping the pain would subside, but it didn't.

"Bina," I said, "I need to go to the toilet."

"Just hold your stomach and it will go away," she said.

But the cramps got worse, and I could no longer hold it in. "Mum!" I shouted. "I need to go to the toilet.

"Bina," Mum called, "go with your sister and leave the hall light on. There is nothing to be afraid of." She was still doing sewing work in the bedroom.

Bina took the torch. We walked out, and stepped cautiously towards the toilet. Bina shone the torch everywhere. Every sound and shadow seemed threatening. As I went into the toilet, Bina stood guard. The toilet had no lights so I kept the door half open.

Bina sat on the stairs. She flashed the torch through the door into the toilet. The toilet was a squat with two stones on both sides for our feet. It took me awhile to get situated, then there was the fear. I'd been in there for almost ten minutes when Bina said: "Come on, hurry up."

"I am," I said.

"Come on," she continued. "I don't feel safe. I will count to fifty. If you won't come out, I will leave."

"I am trying to push but it's not coming," I said. I squeezed my stomach. My legs were getting tired and weak. I felt dizzy. "I will be out in a few minutes. I think it's coming." I pushed my stomach and a tiny hard rock flushed out. I didn't see any light outside the door. "Bina, are you there?"

No reply.

"Bina?" Still no answer. I felt scared. It was too dark. Thoughts of our intruder filled my mind. What if he'd returned, and made off with Bina? I prayed. I was afraid to come out of the toilet. I wanted to cry loud for Papa to come.

Suddenly, a light flashed. *The intruder*, I thought.

Then I heard a voice: "Mila, are you ready?"

"Is that you Bina?"

"Yes," she replied. "Who did you think it was?"

I was angry. "You left me in the dark? I will tell Mum."

Just then I heard a strange sound. "What's that?"

"It's a thundering sound," Bina said.

"It's not a thundering sound," I replied, while pulling up my underwear. Though I was done I was unable to flush. The water tank was too high, and the chain was too short. I jumped a few times, careful not to fall into the toilet. I came out and hit Bina. "You left me in the darkness." The sky showed no sign of rain. As we walked towards the house, I joked, "Someone's behind the coconut tree." We both ran into the house.

Rumbles of thunder always scared us, especially at night. We thought lightning would burst right through the roof and strike us. We were always hearing stories of people who'd been struck by lightning.

CHAPTER 9

That night Bina and I couldn't sleep. We talked until we felt sleepy, and we might've fallen asleep were it not for two big noises: "Bang! Bang!" It was as if something huge had fallen on the road. "What's that?" I cried, my voice waking the others. It was about ten-thirty.

Bina and the two little ones followed me to our parent's room.

"Why are you all here again?" Mum demanded as she continued to work on her sewing.

"Mum," I said, "a big sound scared us."

Mum stopped sewing. "It could be a storm coming. You don't need to be afraid of that." She went back to her work.

"Mum, I want milk," said Kevin.

"Bina, go get warm milk for Kevin."

"BANG! BANG!" The sound came again. Bina dropped the pot and ran back into the room.

Mum had heard this one. She shook Papa, who was fast asleep, snoring loud. "Wake up," she said. "There's a strange sound outside."

"What?" he said in his sleep.

Mum shook him until he woke up.

"I am tired," he mumbled. "I need sleep. No need to worry. We will talk tomorrow morning." He started snoring again.

"We will sleep here, Mum," Kevin said.

She shook her head. "No. This bed is too small for all of us. All of you go to your room."

Papa woke up again. "What's going on?" he asked. "Why are you all over here?"

Mum told Papa about the sound.

"I'll go check it out," he said.

"Be careful," said Mum.

"I won't go too far," he said. He put on his slippers, took the torch and the stick, and left

"Now, all of you go back to your room and let me sleep," Mum insisted. She took Jaimini by her side and lay down. We went to our room and sat on our bed, waiting for Papa to come back. We could hear the squeaking sound of Mum's bed as she turned from side to side. It was almost midnight. We heard the clock ticking. It seemed like every minute was too long. We heard a woman weeping. I opened the window. "What was that?"

"I can't see anything," said Bina.

"Open the window a bit more," said Donna. All of us looked from a half open window.

Kevin stood behind me on a small table. He raised himself up over my head to see outside. "There's Papa." He pointed. Papa was coming back.

Kevin was fidgeting and making noise as Papa came in. Papa went to the bedroom. I told Kevin to quiet down so we could hear what Papa told Mum in the next room.

"As I walked to the front yard, I saw some neighbors gathered under the street light," he said. "'What's going on?' I asked. 'It could be a plane crash,' one man said. 'Look, the sky in the south is much brighter than over here.' 'It can't be,' said another man. 'That's not how it sounds when a plane crashes.'"

Papa went on to tell Mum how everyone was about to go home, when our neighbor, Susan, came out and began complaining that her husband had never returned from work that day. She'd come out thinking her husband was with the crowd.

"Andrew," she'd called. "Andrew. Where could he be?"

Andrew had gone to work that day, but never returned. When his wife, Susan, had heard a scooter, she'd gone running, but it wasn't him. It was a neighbor's son, and she'd asked him: "Have you seen my husband?" The boy had not.

Some of the neighbors had commented on the fact that police officers and government workers still hadn't yet arrived home from their jobs. "Don't worry," they told her. "Go back to your house. He will come back soon." But she had a bad feeling about him. As she got more and more agitated, another woman volunteered to take her home.

In the bedroom of our house Papa told Mum: "I have a bad feeling too. Something is going on out there."

"Oh yeah," Mum said, half asleep, turning on her side. "These Africans like partying. Maybe he is partying with his friends, or maybe he is having an affair. We hear this all the time."

Papa came out and turned off the lights, saying, "You see, there is nothing to be afraid of; this is a regular family drama."

"Let's go to sleep," Bina said, cuddling Kevin.

Kevin pointed. "Look behind you, Mila!"

I froze, then turned slowly.

"There's nothing," Bina laughed. "Kevin is joking." She gave Kevin a light slap on his face. "Don't scare anyone like that ever again."

Finally we all went to sleep.

At three in the morning, I woke up again with another severe stomachache. I lay for a long time, trying to decide whether I should get up. My stomach muscles tightened. I pulled myself up to get an extra blanket, and felt a little dizzy. I laid back, regretting all the fruit I'd eaten. I'd felt like this before, most notably once after having eaten lots and lots of guava. I knew what was coming: my toilet going was blocked for three days.

I have a habit of eating fruit until my stomach feels like bursting. Slowly, I turned on my side, holding my stomach. I crawled into a ball and forced myself to get some sleep. I could hear Papa snoring loudly and outside it was still noisy. I wondered what the outside sounds were, and why it had to happen now.

By three-thirty I was feeling cold and feverish at the same time. I pulled myself up. I felt dizzy again, and thought I was going to throw up there-and-then. An acid taste rose up to my throat. I ran into the kitchen, knelt over the washbasin, and everything from the night before came up. When it was finally over I gorged some water, and lay down on the kitchen floor until I felt cold. I got up, grasped the door and took only the smallest steps. I made it to my bed. By five am I was asleep at last.

I awoke to the creaking of our parents' bedroom door opening. I turned on my side, the blanket half-covering my head as I tried to sleep once more. My stomach still hurt, but less than it had in the night. I heard my mother yawning as she trudged into the bathroom. The cock crowed and the chicks were squealing. It was six am.

Though I still wanted to sleep, I was glad it was finally morning. I thought a hot tea might make me feel better. After finishing in the bathroom, Mum put a huge pot of water on the primus stove. Hearing the sound of the primus, I wished it was teatime, but I knew the rules and traditions of Hindu families: tea would only be served after everyone brushed their teeth and washed.

Mum washed herself and put on a fresh sari, ready to do her chores. She warmed water for each of us to wash with, one at a time. Papa was first.

"Children's father," she called, using their familiar form of address, "the hot water is ready for you."

"I will be there in five minutes, children's mum," he called back to her, falling back into sleep.

Mum poured the steaming water into the bucket, using two kitchen towels to hold the hot pot. In the bathroom she added cold water until it was comfortable, then she called Papa a second time. Papa took the most time getting ready, especially in the bathroom.

This time he answered without hesitation, and went straight into the bathroom. Mum gave Papa his clean clothes for the day. The blue wooden bathroom door had hooks for towels and fresh clothing. You pushed your used clothing into the corner for the daily wash. Papa had a habit of chanting while washing.

Washing in those days meant sitting on a small wooden stool in front of a bucketful of water. You dipped a small can into the bucket, filling it with water, then poured this over yourself.

One by one everyone got ready. "Why is Mila not up yet?" Mum asked from the kitchen. "Mila your hot water is ready. Get up!"

Bina emerged from the bathroom, water still dripping from her hair. In the living room she put on the uniform she'd ironed the night before. She made a loose braid of her hair; she would re-braid it more neatly later. She woke up Donna, then Kevin last of all, and helped them get ready for school.

"Bina," Mum said, "go check on Mila. It's already seven-fifteen. Why is she not up yet?"

Mum's voice seemed especially loud, causing me to cover my head.

Bina came over to me. "Mila, wake up," she said. "You will be late for school. Everyone is ready except you."

Though I was awake, I lacked the strength to stand. I'd hoped to be better by this time, but my whole body was still weak. "I had a rough night," I told Bina. "Stomach problems."

Bina told Mum about my sickness.

"So that's why the whole kitchen smelled this morning," Mum said. "I was wondering who threw up. I had to brush everything with dettol. Everything was sticky." As Mum talked, I could hear her voice loud and clear. "I told her not to eat so many plantains, but she would not listen. Let her sleep. She will take the day off from school." I could hear the clink of cups and dishes as Mum spoke.

By this time Papa had already left. He too was going to school. He was a headmaster, and he always got to his office before the other teachers arrived.

The daylight roused me, and my family's movements were an ongoing disturbance. Little Jaimini was crying.

Mum heated her milk, then set it aside to cool. She picked up Jaimini, who immediately stopped crying.

"Go get Mila for a hot cup of tea," said Mum. "It will make her feel better."

Bina came out to the living room and poked. "Mum wants you in the kitchen," she said.

I plodded into the kitchen and missed something Mum said to me. I felt like I needed to be pampered.

Kevin touched my hair. "You look like an ugly witch," he said, laughing.

"Stop that nonsense," Mum chided him, as she poured tea for me. She pushed the cup slowly towards me. "Here eat a piece of paratha. It will do you good."

I took a bit. I did not feel like eating, but the warm tea made me feel a little better.

"Go back to sleep," Mum said.

Bina left for school, taking Donna and Kevin with her to drop off at Papa's school. I felt sorry that I couldn't give her company that day. Usually Bina and I walked to school together.

CHAPTER 10

As everyone left, our whole house got quiet, and I became aware of sounds from outside. The noise was irritating. Children talked as they walked to school, bicycle bells rang, and the motor on our neighbor, Jeff's, scooter idled as he waited for his wife. Maria instructed Sunday about the day's chores. "Make sure you feed both my sons when they come home for lunch."

I covered my head with the blanket but it didn't help. Sunday kept agreeing with Maria, but I knew that she followed each "yes" with a pinched and ugly expression that she hid.

Finally, after half an hour, the whole neighborhood quieted. Not a single sound could be heard, no chickens, turkeys, or people. Soon the silence was broken by the sounds of Mum washing the clothes in the bathroom. In the hallway Jaimini played with her toys. Mum had an eye on her. I felt my pain receding. As the sun climbed higher I felt warmer, covering myself with only a sheet.

Mum prepared roti dough and put the dal (a lentil soup) on the low flame of the primus. It would slowly cook while she washed the clothing. All that was left to prepare were vegetables, rice, and the rotis. These last tasks were done just before everyone returned home for lunch. That way lunch was always fresh and warm.

At nine am Mum announced: "I should be going to my business. The new girl I hired was supposed to be here fifteen minutes ago. I'd been told that she's always on time, but she is not. It will be better for me to stay home."

As I dozed I could hear Mum talking to herself. "My customers are loyal. Whatever they need, they will come tomorrow."

Mum was in the backyard hanging the wash when she saw the leftover from the night before on the ground. "Extra work for me," she muttered. "I told Bina to throw these away before heading for school." Mum picked up a bucket and walked toward the jackfruit tree. As she climbed over the bend in the fence, she saw the long jute bag. She let it fall open to see what was inside. A leg popped out. Mum dropped her bucket and rushed back to the house, knocking Sunday as the girl came out from the chicken coop with a basket of eggs.

"Can't you see me?" Sunday cried. "Look what you did. All the eggs are broken. My aunty will beat me."

Mum pointed toward the wilderness. "Kuna maiti zaidi ya hapo…" (There is a dead body over there…)

Sunday ran into her house and locked the door. Screaming for help, Mum looked around for a neighbor; there was no one to be seen. *This is unusual*, Mum thought. At this time of the day women are working in their garden or doing some kind of house work. She was alone. The only thing she could do was wait until Papa returned for lunch.

Mum's whole body shook from fear as she also locked herself in the house. She took a break and poured cold water on herself. She sat down in the kitchen, set Jaimini in her lap, and had a cup of tea and a piece of paratha. She dipped a small piece of paratha in the tea and gave it to Jaimini before feeding her a bottle of milk. Mum felt trapped, and thought she had a headache coming on. Unable to concentrate, she'd almost forgotten I was there. She kept seeing the jute bag and the leg. She felt guilty of her ignorance. "I did not listen to what I said a day before."

After a strong tea, she felt better. Remembering I was there, she called: "Mila, come have a cup of tea. You will feel much better."

I lay in a deep sleep full of dreams. The room was crowded. People argued with each other, and there was a lot of noise. Finally I heard Mum's call, and woke up. My petticoat was all wet. I slowly pulled myself up and sat on my bed. The sound was getting louder. *Is this a dream?* I wondered.

The noise came from the street. Bicycle bells rang, scooter engines rumbled, and I realized I'd overslept. It was already ten-thirty and most of the morning was gone. I sat for a moment, still feeling tired. My stomachache was gone. When I stood up my legs were weak.

I kept hearing voices screaming, and it just got louder. In the kitchen Mum was preparing lunch. She'd decided to make an extra dish. The noise from the primus stove and whistle of the pressure cooker blocked any outside sounds.

"Come have a cup of tea, with something to eat," Mum said.

I rubbed my eyes. "Mum, I heard people."

"What people?"

"I don't know," I said.

"Do you feel better now?"

"Yes," I replied.

"The backyard door is locked," she said. "Do not go out."

"Why not?" I asked.

At first she didn't want me to know about the corpse in the jute bag, thinking I would get sick. "It's too hot and it's not good to stand in the sun," she said. "Go and rest until lunch is ready. It is becoming dangerous outside." I protested. That's when she started telling me about her morning chores, the leg in the jute bag and what she went through.

As she talked I walked carefully, heading for the backyard.

"What's going on, Mila?" Sunday asked.

"I don't know," I said. "I heard the noise and I came out."

"There is a dead body over there," she said, pointing.

I looked towards the wilderness. Adrenalin surged through my body.

"Yes, Mum told me." I looked towards the hill, shielding my eyes to see better. Even though my head was getting hot, I didn't move. "What is that?"

People who'd left for work and school were now running down the hill, screaming. As they came closer, I could understand what they were shouting: "They are killing people!"

Blindly they crowded onto the narrow path, jostling, trampling, and climbing over one another. The older and younger folks were getting bruised and cut on the stone path. Finally some brave men helped the weaker ones.

They lifted old women and children and carried them on their backs. As people reached their houses they ran in, locking doors behind them.

Sunday and I looked at each other. I heard a woman weeping, but I didn't bother to look. My eyes were focused on the running crowd.

"Oh, there is Papa!" I cried. "Mum! Mum!"

Mum didn't answer. Kevin was next to Papa, and Donna ran ahead of them. *Where's Bina?* I wondered. The sun warmed my head. I sat down on the stone wall. The banana trees gave me shade.

Finally Mum replied to my calls. "What is it?" she shouted.

"Mum, I saw Papa, Donna and Kevin."

She thought I was joking.

I heard a weeping sound. A bunch of people were gathering at our neighbor, Susan Muheneza's house. I knew her house by the avocado tree she had in her backyard. That day Susan sat on the ground, pounding on her breast. She wept, "Walichukua mume wangu mbali," which meant, they took my husband away.

"What will I do without him?" she cried. "Someone, please help me. What will my children do without their father?"

Another woman cried with her own, similar story. All the women were weeping and pounding their chests.

Though I sympathized, what was I to do? A hand gripped my upper arm and pulled me up. It was Bina. "Get in," she said, nearly dragging me into the house.

"Ow!" I cried. "Don't hold me so tight."

"Don't argue," she said. "Just get inside if you want to stay alive."

"But why is everybody coming back home from school?"

"No time for questions," she snapped. "Get in the house, now."

She'd never spoken to me like that before. I started toward the house, then turned. A lot of our neighbors were already indoors. Papa was slowed by the weight of Kevin on his shoulders, but he didn't stop. He'd always been a good runner, but today he was out of breath when he reached the door.

"Children's mum, come here," he called.

Mum appeared in the hallway holding her rolling pin, and pulling the tangled sari from her waist. She pushed back her hair, leaving white sticky flour on her left cheek and in her hair. "What's going on?" she demanded. "Why are you all back from school?"

Despite her confusion, she started telling him about the leg in the jute bag.

"That should be from last night," said Papa.

"They are killing people!" Kevin and Bina cried.

"What?" said Mum. "Who is killing? And which people?"

"The policeman," Kevin said, but we knew he might be mistaken. Kevin didn't know the difference between a policeman and a soldier. To him, anyone in a uniform was a policeman.

I raised my arm. "I want to know more."

"Quiet, all of you," said Papa as he gasped for breath. "You're making a lot of noise. Mila, Bina, lock all the windows and doors. Children's mum, go finish your cooking as fast as you can. We'll eat whatever's ready." Papa went from room to room, rechecking windows and doors.

"Lunch is ready except the rotis," Mum announced.

"I will roll the rotis, Mum," said Bina.

"I will help you," I volunteered.

As we baked the rotis, I tried to fish more information out of Bina, but she was in shock.

"I don't feel like talking right now," she said.

Once we'd prepared the rotis, we returned to the hallway. That's where Papa wanted us once he'd made sure the doors and windows were locked. This time Mum didn't say a word. She took Jaimini in her lap, gave her a piece of a cookie, and sat there next to Papa. Her dark brown eyes got bigger as she listened. I sat next to her, pulling my knees close, and covering them with my dress. I felt goose bumps on my arms as I listened.

"Where is Donna?" Papa asked. "Did she come in? I saw her running in front of me. She should be here somewhere. So, where is she?"

Mum got mad. "You should've kept an eye on her," she snapped, opening the door and looking out.

"Go find her," said Papa. I searched the kitchen, while Bina looked in the bathroom. Donna was not in either place.

Mum got worried. I stood in the middle of the living room, watching every corner. My gut said she should be there. Then I glimpsed something blue under our bed. "I found her," I shouted.

"How many times have I told you not to shout," Papa said.

I bent down. Donna looked out from her hiding place. She was scared and pale.

"Come," I said softly. "Hold my hand."

Still she was afraid. I took her hand in mine and slowly pulled her out. She crawled to Mum's lap.

Finally we were all quiet. Kevin started. "Can you imagine what we saw? Bodies are scattered all over the road. Yes, Mum, tons of bodies all over on the road." Bina nodded. Donna cried. Mum laid Donna's head on her lap and comforted her.

"Is this really true?" I asked.

"Yes it is," said Papa. "I was in my office with three other teachers when a lorry full of soldiers, each carrying a loaded rifle, stopped in front of our school. One big man jumped from the front seat and came straight into my office. He broke open the door, while the others surrounded the school. His dark skin glistened as sweat dripped on his uniform. He looked at everyone, then came to our table, aiming his gun at Mrs. Desouza's head. She cried, "I didn't do anything, please don't kill me!". The man pressed the rifle to her neck. "That hurts, please don't kill me!" "School's over!" he told us. "Tell your students to go home. The curfew will start this evening."

"Mrs. Desouza shook and perspired. The other teachers looked down. I had the responsibility of protecting them and their students. I stood up. 'What's going on, my friend?' I asked. "

"He pushed the rifle to my neck. It hurt."

"Were you scared, Papa?" Kevin interrupted.

"Yes," Papa replied. "At first, I thought he was going to kill me the way he pushed the rifle. These people are crazy. I took a deep breath. Again the soldier pressed the rifle hard on my neck. He told me not to question him. I didn't, and he left."

"What happened next?" I asked.

"Well, you know Mrs. Desouza.... She panicked, and started blubbering, 'How will I go home? They are everywhere.' Mrs. Shah was frightened too. Mrs. Shah gave her a glass of water and told her they would find someone to escort them to their houses."

We knew Mrs. Shah. She was a wise and a brilliant teacher who got up every morning at five am to meditate. She'd learned the peace mantras from her late grandmother. Every Thursday evening she opened her house to others who came to chant together.

Papa told us how Mrs. Dezousa had relaxed, then took out her handkerchief. She wiped her tears and blew her nose. She then packed her belongings and waited in the office.

"Don't you worry, Mrs. Shah," Papa said. "I will call Hassan. He has to take the same road to his house. He will escort Mrs. Dezousa and you to your houses."

Papa instructed the rest of the teachers to notify their students about the curfew. "Tell them to pack their belongings and go straight to their houses," he said. "They should not roam around in the town or in any fields."

Then Papa checked every classroom to see if anyone was left. That's when he got Donna and Kevin. He explained that there would be a curfew, and that he would tell them about that later.

They left an almost empty school. The school concierge Martin, had locked himself and his wife Elizabeth into their small room, but they were the only ones left. Martin and Elizabeth were a happily newly wedded couple. Martin was the school janitor. Elizabeth a house woman. They lived at the back of the school. The same lorry was still parked at the corner of the school compound. The soldiers were announcing that the curfew would start that evening, and we were all supposed to go to our houses. On the way home, Papa, Kevin and Donna saw more soldier-filled lorries parked on every street. Bodies lay everywhere on the roads and in the grass. It was party time for the vultures with as much fresh meat as they wanted.

When Donna saw these things, she wept uncontrollably. Papa had to carry her part of the way. At the shopping street, storekeepers were closing their businesses. They had opened as usual, not knowing what was coming. People ran screaming past the stores, knocking down their displays. Astounded, some pulled their displays inside, pulling down the shutters and the iron grill, they locked themselves in their houses. Every shop had a backhouse with a garden connected with their business. Everywhere people ran, like chickens escaping the chopping block.

Papa hadn't known that I'd been sick, so my absence worried him, but he knew all he could do was head for home.

CHAPTER 11

Bina interrupted Papa with her story. Her school's headmaster, a tall white Englishman, Mr. Dickens, came into each classroom, telling teachers and students to pack up and go home. At first Bina and her friends liked the thought of leaving school. Then they saw the soldiers. Mr. Dickens cooled their panic and told them to get their belongings. He then marched them, one-by-one, out into the crowded hallway.

The hallway was like a train station full of overwhelmed and hurrying people. Bina ran towards the front entrance, then stopped when she saw the soldiers' lorry. "I thought of my friend, Dina," she told us. "I was too scared to go home all by myself and wished Mila was with me. I missed her."

Bina went back to look for Dina in her classroom. It was empty. Bina got mad, wondering how her friend could leave without her. She asked the first classmate she saw if he'd seen Dina. He'd seen her running. Bina didn't know what to do. Finally a teacher yelled at her: "Do not just stand there, Bina! Go home!" When Bina looked into one last classroom, a soldier saw her through the window. She nearly peed her pants. She walked, then ran, dropping some of her books. But she didn't run home yet.

She finally found her friend in the bathroom, too scared to even get up from the toilet seat.

"Come, we must go," Bina said, pulling Dina up.

"I can't," Dina replied.

"Why not?"

Dina had no answer. She was so stiff that Bina had to pull her every step of the way. With her attention on Dina, Bina bumped into a pillar and hurt her head. She was bleeding, and felt as if she might faint, but a voice inside her head shouted, "Run for your life!" Taking Dina with her, she did just that. Taking short cuts, they still had to travel roads littered with bodies. Some were badly beaten up; some had their necks hanging loose and hollow places where their eyes had been, like zombies. Eagles and flies were already feasting on them. Bina felt like vomiting but kept on running, still pulling Dina with every step.

"Just focus on your house," Bina told her friend. "We've already made it. Only a few meters to go."

Finally they were there. Luckily the front metal gate was wide open. Dina banged on her front door. The moment her mother opened it, Dina fainted.

"Oh! My little baby!" cried her mother. Bina told Dina's mother what had happened, then said she had to go home.

"Why don't you stay at our house until Dina's father comes home," Dina's mother offered. "He will drive you home."

Bina refused. "It's only fifteen minutes away," she said. Bina didn't feel comfortable and wanted to be home safely with her family.

Dina's mother told Bina to walk with any groups she saw. Bina left. As she reached the main road, she saw a group across the road from the church and caught up with them. They kept their eyes cast downward.

The main road from Kampala to Entebbe was blocked. Three lorries full of soldiers watched the civilians as they headed for their homes. A big soldier with a megaphone stood on the back of a lorry announcing the curfew. Bina's group walked slowly towards the church until they were out of the soldiers' line of vision, then they all started running again.

Bina felt safer when she saw Papa in the distance. She called, but he didn't hear. She ran, and finally caught up with him. He wanted to know where I was. Bina told him I'd stayed at home.

Bina's forehead was bruised and bleeding, so Mum got cotton and a match. Mum always used ayurvedic* medicine.* She lit the cotton and let it burn out as she tapped it lightly on Bina's forehead. "This will stop the bleeding and your skin will recover faster," she said.

***

We locked ourselves in the house for three days. In the evenings, we used old-fashioned kerosene lanterns. During the day the sunlight from the crack beneath the backdoor was enough to see by. Nobody in our neighborhood dared to keep bright lights on in the evenings. Every street was still and every house was silent, whether it was day or night. It was as if everyone had moved out, leaving only emptiness behind. The only

---

*It is a traditional system of treatment originating from India; known as Ayurvedic medicine.

sounds came from a distance: the squawking of hens and turkeys, the steady song of the grasshoppers, and the occasional trauma of gunfire.

That day Papa could not wait to hear the latest news. He got up and went to the radio by the bed. We were too scared to sit in the hallway by ourselves. Someone might burst through the front door and shoot us at any moment. We followed Papa.

Papa sat on the side of the bed by the night table, holding the radio. The rest of us gathered around Mum. In silence we watched as Papa's fingers turned the knobs. Reception was spotty at best. This irritated Papa, but he wouldn't give up. Finally he found Radio Uganda. Though the voices came through only erratically, we could figure out what we were hearing.

Papa leaned in close, putting his ear to a speaker. We waited anxiously.

"I should clean up in the kitchen," said Mum.

"Shhh," said Papa. "Listen." It was a man's voice. He was speaking to the whole nation. He said:

"My name is Erinayo Oryeman. I am the Inspector General of Police. This message is to inform the people of Uganda that the government has been taken over by military force."

At those words, silence fell over everyone. The nation's future seemed to hang in the balance. The message seemed to be that of fear.

A few hours later we heard the words of an army officer who supported the coup. He said: "The government of Uganda has been taken over. I repeat; the government of Uganda has been taken over, and any interfering force will be crushed." When people heard this they feared what was to come.

Another thick, northern west Nile accent voice followed. "Thank you," he said. "Thank you very much. I am his Excellency General Idi Amin Dada. I am your new president for life. I am not a politician. I am a professional soldier. I am here to make Uganda a better place.

"Friends, relatives and distinguished guests, I am happy to have you all here today, to celebrate the country's liberation. Uganda is now a free country."

Cheers and applause came through the radio speaker.

"The military government will remain as a caretaker regime until new elections. These will be announced when the situation is normalized. I promise to release all political prisoners.

"I must remind you, my government will not tolerate politicians, or anyone else who tries to defeat me and my government."

Suddenly Amin started laughing. He told jokes, then got down to business again: "Obey me and no harm will be done to you. Those who will not listen will be severely punished. All Obote's men are traitors. Obote's government has been corrupted. He has given preferential treatment to the Lango region in the north part of the country and his policies are leading to bloodshed. They do not deserve to live. I will make sure to clean up the mess Obote has made of this country. Thank you, thank you... So long, so long..." He said those things over and over.

From the radio we heard cheering and applause, then gunfire in honor of Uganda's new dictator. Suddenly the sounds from the radio stopped, yet we could still hear cheers and music. Despite the curfew, many people were still out in the streets of Kampala.

Papa wore a thoughtful expression. We said nothing, waiting for him to speak. "Everything will be fine," he said. "You don't need to worry as long as I am with you."

"What do you mean?" Mum demanded, raising her hands to her head. "What are we going to do? Where will we go?"

At the same time Kevin cried out: "Yippie! No school! I can play as much as I want to!"

None of us agreed with his optimism.

"How could this happen?" Mum muttered. "Who is this Idi Amin, who adds 'Dada' to his name? Obote was a good man. We never had any problem with him."

"It's all politics and power," Papa said. "Obote made the mistake of promoting this man, Amin, and Amin has gained the support of the army. He is not educated nor intelligent, but he's a strong, fast warrior, and a heavyweight boxing champion with Kakwa and Lugbara blood. Obote trusted him at first, then, as Amin's power grew, he got more and more greedy. Obote had no choice. Right now Obote is at a Commonwealth meeting in Singapore. That's given Amin this chance, and he's taken over."

"But it all seems so sudden," Mum said.

"Not really," said Papa. "Do you recall when the Congo was in turmoil?"

"Oh, yes," Mum said. "How could I forget? The natives were knocking on everyone's door, selling gold for less than it was worth. I bought some."

"And that was when Obote gave Amin the opportunity to establish his personal fortune," said Papa. "Then Obote wanted to aid the rebels who were losing their fight against the new government of Mobutu. Obote bypassed the army commander, Opolot, and put Amin in charge of getting arms and transport to the rebels. Amin took advantage of this to extort truckloads of gold and ivory the rebels had seized as they'd retreated.

Mum sat on the bed. Holding both her fingers together, she said. "We didn't hear any of these before." All these years we felt safe."

"Obote made other mistakes. He imprisoned his political opponents without trial. With Amin now in full command of the army, Uganda was ripe for military dictatorship. Obote was probably getting ready to remove Amin, and Amin probably knew it. That's how all this happened."

Papa was right. President Milton Obote had been arranging for General Amin and his army supporters to be arrested by loyal Langi officers, but someone leaked this to Amin. On the evening of January 24, 1971, Amin contacted a few of his most trusted officers and told them to take over the armories. With just a few tanks, his forces took over the radio station, and that's how we were able to hear his speech.

At Entebbe Airport, early morning travelers were evacuated. Some stayed with the two Roman Catholic priests in the airport waiting room. They were killed. Amin's forces sealed off the Entebbe International airport, surrounded the president's residence, and blocked the major roads from Kampala to Entebbe. They then started hunting down officer's still loyal to Obote.

CHAPTER 12

After our horrible night I finally slept. When I awoke I could still hear the fearful sounds coming from somewhere outdoors. Papa was still getting what news there was from the radio. Donna was cold, so Mum dressed her in a warm sweater and gave her an aspirin. There was nothing we could do.

When it was time for lunch we ate without saying a word to each other. After lunch Mum took Donna to her bedroom. Donna was running a severe fever and it was getting worse. Papa followed them while, Bina and I cleaned up the kitchen. Unlike other times, we didn't sing, laugh, or throw soap at one another. We just cleaned and made as little noise as possible. Like Papa and Mum, we children also got worried.

Staying locked up indoors was strange. We were children. We needed to run and play in the fresh air. Instead we were trapped between four walls, our freedom gone.

Papa spent the day trying to get news from the radio and the TV. He tried every station, and listened to every word. The main roads between Entebbe and Kampala were still blocked and soldiers were everywhere. On TV the image was blurry and the sound was fuzzy. Our antenna had been damaged in a storm a week earlier.

"Make sure you keep the volume low," Mum cautioned.

We watched the wavering onscreen images, and listened to the voices that came from the speakers. In Kampala, crowds cheered and waved as Amin rode through, armed soldiers flanking him on each side of his

open jeep. Tanks followed. Traditionally dressed drummers played Djembe and Ngoma. Also conforming to tradition, ladies went topless, but covered their thighs in grass tutu dresses to perform a tribal dance. The rest of the women were dressed in colorful gomesi.

Finally Amin arrived, and he danced up the red carpet to the stage. His sons were with him, and his wives were close behind. He stopped, shook his butt in a dance, and touched some of the ladies.

"You are beautiful," he said to each one. "What's your name?" Each woman was infected by his charm.

He wore his full dress uniform, studded with medals. All around him Ugandan flags flew, with their bands of black, yellow, and red. The grey-crowned crane in the middle was a symbol of a gentle nature. He was surrounded by body guards and his people.

As his wives and sons took their seats ahead of the politicians, Amin took the stage. The National anthem played. When the music ended he started speaking. He declared himself king of Scotland, believing he was that country's king. Among his audience were British officials who'd known him for years. They were aware of his reputation for brutality. They also knew how manipulative and duplicitous he could be. Yet there was no way for them to guess what was coming. Amin would soon be ordering atrocities that most would find unimaginable.

His speech wasn't long. He promised the curfew would soon end. He saw a bright future. He wanted everyone to pay attention to the news reports from his radio station. There he would announce any and all changes to his policies and decrees. "Make sure you all listen to the news every day," he said, pointing at the crowd. He laughed, put his hand on his son's head, waved good bye, and said, "So long, so long." Then he was gone.

As we watched and listened, we couldn't see what was ahead. In the coming months Amin would actually improve Uganda's business climate, seeming to give non-citizens reason to feel relieved. He offered residence permits, and said he welcomed imported goods. The Asian business community began to bring their money and assets back into Uganda, and for a short time the nation's economy grew. Yet even in those early days we feared the truth. We'd seen what his soldiers could do.

On the day that Amin took power, we were still children playing games. Our favorite was Ludo, a board game closely related to Parcheesi. We spent the afternoon playing it in the hallway.

To us the curfew had unexpected advantages. Papa was so wrapped up in watching and listening to the news that he didn't even think of giving us homework. That left us with plenty of time to play our favorite indoor game.

One day at five pm, Mum went into the kitchen. "I will start preparing dinner," she said.

"This early?" asked Bina. "Do you want me to help?"

"No, I will prepare something simple before it gets dark. What worries me is the kerosene. We have very little left. We have to be a bit stingy with the lanterns burning."

Mum had an early dinner ready for us at six pm. When night fell we kept playing Ludo in the light of our bedroom lantern. Our time in the closed-up house was beginning to affect us. When I started winning, Bina and Kevin got jealous. Foolishly I smiled and acted as if I might be hiding something. Then they accused me of cheating.

"We won't play with you anymore," they told me. Just as I agreed to stop, we all fell silent. Outside a vehicle was approaching. *Who on the earth?* we wondered.

When Mum heard it she opened a window just a crack, and we pushed each other to get a look outside. In the nearby homes our neighbors were doing the same thing. It was a lorry carrying a dozen soldiers. It rolled to a stop right across the road.

Mum told Donna and Kevin: "Both of you go back to bed."

Neither of them moved.

We watched as soldiers dropped from the lorry and surrounded Mr. Zachary Okella's house. Mr. Okella lived there with his wife and son. The sergeant, a tall chubby man, kicked the Okellas' front door. When it didn't fly open, the sergeant stepped back and ordered another soldier to help. When both of them kicked the door, it flew open.

Mr. Okella had come home from work and gone into his bedroom to rest. Hearing the commotion, he came into the living room just as the sergeant started pounding against the door.

As Mr. Okella opened his mouth to protest, he heard, "Zinazunguka nyumba na kuua bastad Langi afisa!" They were calling to each other to surround the house and "kill this bastard Langi official."

Mr. Okella realized these were Amin's troops. He had only seconds to act. His wife, Alice, cradled their baby son. He pushed them both beneath the table and ran back into the bedroom. He was about to jump out the window when he saw soldiers in the backyard. He stepped behind the curtains just as the soldier entered the house.

Alice put her hand on her son's mouth and prayed: "God help my family." She could see a soldier's boots from under the table. *What is going on?* she wondered. *What has my husband done?*

The sergeant searched in the closet, under the bed, and in the bathroom and kitchen. "He is not here!" he cried. "This tiny house doesn't have many hiding places. I think he must've escaped."

One of the other soldiers started grabbing expensive artwork and pushed it into a large bag.

"Let's go," said the sergeant.

"I'm coming," the soldier replied. They were about to exit when Alice's baby cooed.

"What was that?" the sergeant asked, stopping. "I think I heard something."

The baby cooed again. Alice put her hand to her son's mouth, but he kept making noise.

The soldier went to the table and pulled up the tablecloth. "Tafadhali don't kutuua," she kept repeating, begging them not to kill her and her child. The soldier grabbed her shoulder, and pulled her upright.

The sergeant came in. "Aha," he said, "married to Acholi." The new regime was banning marriages between the Acholi tribe and the Lugbara tribe, though these people all lived together. "Where is your husband?" the sergeant demanded, pointing the rifle barrel at her.

"He is not home," she said, looking down at her baby.

"Don't lie to us," he threatened. "We won't kill you because you are our tribe, but we will kill your baby. Where is your husband hiding?"

Alice covered her baby's face. They pulled her by her hair and put a pistol to her son's face.

"I do not know," she wept. "Please don't kill us. Tumefanya kitu kibaya!" *We have done nothing wrong!*

"Go check the bedroom again," the sergeant ordered. He stayed with Alice, still threatening to kill her child.

Finally one soldier called out: "Sisi kupatikana mwanaharamu!" *We found the bastard!*

Mr. Okella had hidden. They pulled him out and dragged him into the living room. He was scared to death. "I didn't do anything," he protested. "I am a good honest citizen. Please let me go."

One soldier smacked Alice's face and threw her on the floor, kicking her.

"Please," Mr. Okella pleaded, "take me but leave my

wife alone!"

The soldiers turned their attention to him. They kicked him and battered him with rifle butts until he could no longer stand. He asked for mercy. They dragged him outside and threw him on the grass. Finally they tossed him in the back of the lorry and drove away.

Alice crawled outside after the lorry left. Battered and bleeding, she cried for help. No one dared to go to her. We felt terrible, but so far she and her baby had survived. Perhaps they would escape the fate of Mr. Okella.

These soldiers were hunting down Langli and Acholi tribe members still faithful to Obote. Amin felt that all Obote followers must be spies. The penalty was death. What we'd witnessed was Uganda's new reality. We did not feel good that evening.

When the curfew was lifted, and we could come out again, we heard from Alice they'd pulled out Mr. Okella's tongue, cut his ears off, then thrown him into the Nile to be eaten by crocodiles.

On the night of Mr. Okella's abduction Donna had nightmares. "How many times have I told you not to look at these kinds of things, but you won't listen," said Mum. "Now all of you go to sleep. I need a strong cup of chai. I am getting headaches." She headed for the kitchen.

The next day we got up late. There was nothing to do but cook, eat or clean the kitchen. When we heard someone creeping through our backyard, we peeked through the curtain and saw Sunday sneaking into the chicken coop to feed the birds. She came back out with a dozen freshly laid eggs.

It reminded me of better times a year before. Mum had

bought a chicken for fresh eggs. Each time the chicken laid an egg, it ate it. Finally Papa said to Sunday: "Will you slaughter this chicken?" She agreed to do it, and the rest of us watched. She chopped the chicken's head off, and the body ran headless into the wilderness. Sunday finally caught it, and Papa made a delicious chicken curry for our lunch that day.

Now we couldn't run outdoors at all.

Early the next morning our neighbor, Maria, knocked on the kitchen wall. Mum and Papa were careful. "Maria…" Mum called, and at the same time Papa peered through the crack of the window overlooking the front yard. "There is nobody out there," he said.

A moment later Maria appeared in her hallway.

"Is everything all right?" Mum asked, holding her ear towards the wall.

"Oh! Mrs. Saita," she replied, "I have lots of fresh eggs for you. Usually, I give them to my friends on the other side of the area."

"Okay," said Mum. "I'll come pick them up." Mum looked this way and that, then, once she felt it was safe, she rushed over to the neighbor's door. There she picked up a basket full of eggs and some sweet potatoes. "This will be a good dinner," she murmured moments later as she came back into our house."

That evening, while Mum, the vegetarian, ate some leftovers, we had eggs with sweet potatoes for dinner.

During the long curfew the only time we left the house was to go to the toilet. We went in the evenings, Papa escorting us. He would stand outside holding a stick to ward off any threats.

One evening, as we sat playing Ludo in the hallway

close to our parent's door, there came a knock on the back door. We froze. Somewhere a shadow moved, and we heard a second knock.

"Who is it?" Papa called.

We heard a voice, but no words.

"I can't hear you," said Papa.

"Please let me in," said a man's voice.

"Who are you?" Papa asked again.

Instead of replying, the man knocked harder. Papa picked up his stick and pushed aside the curtain. An African man looked in at him.

Papa recognized him. "It's Andrew Odwe." Papa quickly opened the door.

Mr. Odwe entered limping; he was about to fall down. Papa helped him into a chair. "He's Andrew, children," said Papa.

As we peered from behind the door at this scary sight, Papa asked Andrew: "Where have you been? Oh God! What happened to your eye? It's gone." It was gouged out. "That is grizzly," said Bina, putting her hands over Kevin's eyes. Papa got a glass of water and a towel. Andrew's body was covered with bruises and cuts. He was tired and unable to talk much. He kept mumbling that he wanted to go home.

Papa pulled a chair up next to him. "I will take you home, but first, tell me what happened. I've heard your wife is worried over your absence."

We peeked out, watching as Andrew drank the water and put the towel to his left eye. He spoke from deep in his throat: "The Lugbara and Kakwa are slaughtering all Acholi and Langi because of their links to Obote. Two days ago, I came out of my office. Two men approached me. They grabbed me by my arms and dragged me. They beat me and stabbed me before pushing me into a car. I cried for them to let me go. They covered my head and face with a black cloth. When I asked them what they were doing, they wouldn't reply. I screamed, but no help came. They hit my head with their fits, drove me down a bumpy road, then pushed me into a small dark place with other men.

"Most of us were ordinary civil servants. I was kept there for one-and-a-half days, while they dragged in fifteen more, mostly young men shouting and screaming to get out. They stopped when they realized it wouldn't help. We were all afraid. The next day they said they were transferring us to a nicer place. All the men from the Baraka were put into a military convoy.

"I requested that the man in charge let me go home. I told him of my worried wife and small children. The man didn't care; he was obeying his orders. His hateful face showed no mercy to anyone. Dressed up in an soldier's uniform, his shout was shrill, 'Nobody talks to me like this, especially you! You are Obote's men. You don't deserve to live.'

"When I shouted and screamed, he told his men: 'Give this man special treatment.' They drove us near the lake, where they pushed out all the men except me and two others. I saw a pile of bodies, and at that moment, I realized they'd brought us there to kill us. 'Run!' I shouted to my African brothers. 'Run!' They all ran but were shot. The soldiers forced me and the other two to gather the bodies, adding them to the pile. They then poured kerosene on the bodies and set them on fire. I was shaky. I cried. These were innocent young men with wives and children. They had not harmed anyone. Today, their wives are widows and their children are without fathers. What a brutality to our own black people!

"They told the other two to strip off their clothing, then they made me tie them to a tree. 'My brothers,' I said as I did it, 'forgive me. God be with all of us.' The soldiers chopped off one the men's penis and another one's ear's and left them there to die. They then covered my face with the black cloth and drowned me. Before I could die they removed the cloth from my head. Two men held me, and the other one took out his knife and removed my left eye. It was very painful. I screamed. I said to myself, 'this is it. My life is ending.' I thought of my wife and children. I prayed. My nose, eye and mouth were all bleeding. I went limp. When they threw me into the water I floated among the other corpses, pretending I was dead. Holding tight to a corpse, I somehow managed to stay afloat and breathe. The water was reddish with blood from the many bodies. It was dawn. I was going into shock. I kept on thinking of good memories of my wife and children just to keep me awake. I needed to stay alive for them. I could hear them on the lakeshore laughing and talking. One of them took out a cigarette and they shared it. I shivered, and knew my pulse was slowing.

"Because I am a very good swimmer, I guess, I survived. I was the lucky one who'd lived. When they were out of sight I hung onto one of the bodies, and swam to shore. Once I got out I lay down on the grass, unable to move. I was falling into sleep when I heard a car coming. I got so scared that I crawled towards the tree where I wanted to free the other two. One was dead, but the other was still breathing. I managed to get him loose. We limped away from the lake, not knowing where we were going. There was a sugar plantation close by. A good hiding place. We stayed on the sugar plantation through the night, and before morning the other man died. The next day a worker on his bicycle saw something moving. He saw me eating the sugar cane. I got scared and tried to walk away. Stop, he said. I won't hurt you. He told me to stay in hiding until his friend came. This friend would take me home.

"Early that evening a blue car stopped on the dirt road near the plantation. They took me in the trunk, and dropped me in the fields near my house. At first, I felt as if I was lost. There was not much of a hiding place here except a few small bushes and trees. I was unable to climb the tree. I sat between the bushes. Though I longed to see my wife and children, I stayed there until it got dark. I was very tired, hungry and thirsty and it was getting cold I mean really cold. The sound of splashing water on the lakeshore seemed much closer by. It helped me rejuvenate. I knocked at one of the houses, but no one opened, so I came to this one. I knocked on your door thinking it was my house."

Papa pulled Andrew up from his chair and helped the limping man out. Papa called our neighbor, Godfrey, who opened his back door. "What is it, Babu?" Godfrey called."

"I need a hand," said Papa.

When Godfrey was too scared to come out, his wife, Maria got angry. "Go help Babu," she said. "You see, Babu helps everyone."

At the sound of her angry voice Godfrey came out.

They carried Andrew to his house, watching to be sure no one was following.

Godfrey laid Andrew at the door. "I am going," he said.

"You stay until we are sure his wife can take care of her husband," Papa ordered. Papa tapped on the door, calling, "I am your neighbor, Mr. Babu." When there was only silence Papa kept knocking, but no one opened the door. Papa moved Andrew closer to the door. The injured man called, "Susan, Susan, it's me. Andrew."

Hearing her husband's voice, his wife opened the door. She wept at her husband's condition. "Ambapo umekuwa upendo wangu," she said, asking, *Where have you been my love?* "I was told by one of your colleagues, you were taken away. I am so glad you are alive." She brought some fresh towels and warm water to clean him up. She thanked Papa and Godfrey.

Andrew stayed with his wife and children for two days, and then went into hiding. After that he sometimes came at night to visit his family.

CHAPTER 13

Eventually Amin lifted the curfew, and we were able to go back to school and get on with our lives. The streets were cleaned, the stores opened, and people returned to work. After a couple of weeks of peace, we began to forget the violence. It might have been completely erased from our memories had people not begun disappearing. Those of the Langli and Acholi tribes started vanishing one-by-one.

As our world went back to normal, Papa returned to his after-school tutoring. One of his students was the son of Dr. Obote's closest family member. One day, when Papa was waiting for a taxi into Kampala, a man stopped his car and gave him a lift. Papa thanked him for his generosity. The man introduced himself as Brigadier General Ojite, President Obote's top military man. On their way to Kampala, both of them talked about their families and the schools their children were attending.

"My son, John, is not doing very well in school," Ojite said. "He's often sick.

"If you want, I'll tutor him," said Papa without hesitation.

So Papa began going to Ojite's house once a week after school. He tutored John for almost two months. Then came three days in a row when John wasn't in school.

Papa went to their house, knocked on the door and Ojite's wife Helen answered.

"Babu," she said, "I am glad you came. Come in, have a seat."

Papa sat down and found himself shivering. The house was unusually cold. "What's going on?" he asked.

But Helen was already calling her husband, "Ojite, Babu is here."

Ojite came out from his bedroom and greeted Papa.

"I came to find out what's going on," said Papa. "John did not show up to school for the last three days."

"Yes," said Ojite. "My son is very sick. He has tuberculosis and, according to the doctors, he has only three months to live." Tears ran down the father's cheeks as he spoke of his son.

"Where is John?" Papa asked.

"Come," said Ojite, and he escorted Papa to John's bedroom.

John, a skinny pale boy, lay still. He looked up, greeted Papa, and then said, "I am sorry, sir. I can't take tutoring anymore." He closed his eyes.

Papa laid his hand on the boy's head. "I wish you good health."

"Take rest, my son," said John's father, and both men walked out.

Out in the living room, Ojite offered Papa a seat, and called to his wife to make tea.

"This is very sad," Papa said. "I was just getting to know John. I had a feeling there was something going on with him, but I couldn't figure out what it was. After a couple of tutoring sessions he began to do better in school."

"Yes, he was fine until a week ago," Ojite said. "But then he started losing a lot of weight, and he got weaker. We took him to see a doctor. That's when we learned the truth."

"Please listen," said Papa. "Your son will soon get well. You and Mrs. Ojite need to have faith and pray."

Ojite looked at Papa, thinking, *What is Babu talking about?* Out loud he asked: "How is that possible? The doctors already made their prognosis."

"Miracles can help your son," Papa replied. He urged Ojite and Helen to find courage, then he left for home.

The next day, Papa returned with Saibaba's vibhuti* and some incense. He told Ojite to burn incense every day with their prayers. He also wanted them to put a pinch of vibhuti in their son's mouth, or rub it on his forehead every day. After Ojite and Helen had followed these instructions for a couple of weeks, John began getting better. As his improvement continued, his parents saw it as a miracle. They were grateful to have met a good friend like Papa. It's all about putting intention out there, Papa said.

Almost six weeks after Papa's last visit, he arranged with Ojite to come to their house to see how John was doing. The boy would need to do a lot of catching up in every school subject.

When Papa got there he knocked on the door. No one came. Papa knocked again. Still nothing. He stood there for fifteen minutes. "Ojite knows I'm coming," he said to himself. "Where could they have gone?" Kampala was the only possibility Papa could think of, but why would they take John there? The boy was still weak. He should've

---

*Sacred ash from the burning of certain wood.

been at home, under the care of others.

Papa walked around the side of the house. The living and the bedroom curtains were drawn shut in the windows. In the back he could see inside through a kitchen window. There was a loaf of bread and some food on the kitchen table. The plates and cups were set as if for dinner.

"Ojite!" Papa called. "Ojite, are you home?"

Someone from the neighboring house looked out from a window.

Papa walked towards the window. "Is anyone here? I am the headmaster from Entebbe primary school. I am here to tutor your neighbor's son, John."

An older lady appeared in the window, and gestured for Papa to come closer.

"Why are you hiding? What's going on?" Papa asked.

"No one is home there," the old lady said, pointing at the empty house.

"So where are they?" Papa asked.

"I don't know," she replied. "Yesterday evening, when my grandson went to play with John, he heard Ojite telling Helen to pack the necessary things as fast as she could. He said they would be going into hiding as soon as darkness fell. He no longer felt safe. They are killing Obote's people, and Ojite seemed to think he was next on their list. When my grandson told me all this, I ignored him, but this morning when we woke up, they were gone."

"I was just getting to know them," Papa said sadly. He thanked the lady, and left.

Later we heard that Amin's men had found Ojite hiding in a hut in one of the nearby villages. They took him away, stripped his clothes off, tied him to a tree, and whipped him until his back was bleeding. They cut off his ears, pulled out his tongue, then cut him into small pieces. We had no idea whether his family had survived. We heard rumors. Idi Amin freezes his enemies to be eaten by him.

Like so many other things we learned, this only made us sad.

CHAPTER 14

By late that year Bina and I had finished elementary school, and we were ready to begin secondary school. Because Entebbe had no secondary schools, our only option was to find a school in Kampala. Papa applied at different schools, and one of them accepted both Bina and me.

I was excited. I would be leaving this small town and going into the big city. I wondered how life would be different there, and what adventures I would have. I would make new friends, and learn how people lived in the city.

Bina and I got new socks, shoes, uniforms, books and other school items. The evening before our first day we ironed our short black skirts and white blouses, then polished our shoes. The next morning, we got up an hour earlier than usual. Before we went to catch a taxi on the main road, Mum warned us to be careful and not to talk to strangers.

Our new blue sweaters kept us warm in the morning chill. Ten minutes passed. A couple of taxis went by, loaded with passengers. The third one stopped at the curb. It had three vacant seats.

"You go first," said Bina.

I squeezed myself into a seat next to a man. I didn't dare look around, but I watched from the corner of my eye.

Bina took the window seat. "Kampala taxi stand," she told the driver. These were the only words either of us spoke on that ride. Bina and I were the only Indians in the taxi. The rest of the passengers were Africans. As we headed toward Kampala, the narrow road stretched into the valley like a long, reddish carpet. The road passed through green fields and maize plantations, as well as Native-owned stalls selling fruits and drinks close to the road. Ladies in their colorful gomesis walked barefoot alongside the road, babies tied to their backs, as they carried baskets of fruits on their heads. Bicyclists carried as many as three or four big green banana loops.

Our first stop was Makerere College on the outskirts of Kampala. One day I hoped to study there. By the time we approached Kampala the taxi was full. Whenever someone got out another passenger boarded. Soon the whole taxi smelled of passengers' perspiration.

We all got out at the main taxi stand in Kampala. Bina and I went to the main road and waited for a bus. It arrived and took us to school. We returned home the same way, not having any time to explore the city. We got home at six pm.

One night the following January, as Mum checked the windows before going to bed, she heard someone screaming. In the light from the road Mum saw someone run from a nearby house, then disappear in the darkness. She thought little of it. She was tired, so she went to bed.

The following morning neighbors had gathered in front of the house in question.

"Bina, come look," I called. We both looked out from the living room window. Papa came in and watched with us.

"I will go check it out after I get ready," he said.

"Can I come too?" I asked.

"No," he replied. "You both need to get ready for school."

His answer failed to satisfy my stubborn curiosity, so I waited until he was in the bathroom and snuck outside.

"What's going on?" I asked a huge lady with facial hair and a big head wrap.

She pointed at one of the houses. "Mr Businge's wife was having an affair with someone living there." Her voice was deep like a man's. "Yesterday evening Mr. Businge came back from work early and found his wife wasn't home. He'd suspected she might be having an affair with our neighbor, Akili."

She went on to explain that Mr. Businge, a Langi who was known as sensible, moral and hardworking, was fed up with his wife's behavior. He went straight to Akili's house, and knocked open the back door, shouting, "How can you do this to me?" At the sound of Mr. Businge's voice, his wife screamed. He pulled her away from there, and dragged her back to their house. There he locked her in a room, picked up an axe and ran back to Akili's house. He grasped Akili's hand.

"Please don't," begged Akili. "Please let me go."

But Mr. Businge was beyond reason. He raised the axe and chopped off Akili's right arm, and left him there. A neighbor found Akili early this morning, collapsed in his doorway. Now an ambulance took him to the hospital.

I ran back to our house with this grisly tale. I locked our door, turned, and there stood Papa.

"I told you not to go out," he said. "Get going to school right now." He lightly slapped my head.

I put on my shoes, picked up my books and headed towards the main road with Bina.

"So what was that all about?" Bina asked.

"Oh! Our neighbor's wife was having an affair. So her husband chopped off her lover's hand."

Bina shivered. "It is terrifying," she said.

That evening, Mum spoke of hearing the scream, and seeing someone running the night before.

As incidents like these increased, our parents grew worried. They decided we should move to Kampala, where we would be closer to our new school. Papa got a teaching position in one of Kampala's schools. In March we took a four-room apartment above some storage units overlooking a huge taxi stand. The stand was surrounded by retail stores. Ours was one of four apartments, each one sharing the same stairways down to the road walk.

There was a nearby bus stand, and we could get to school in twenty minutes. That allowed us to sleep later. Also, there in the city we felt far more secure. We made new friends and started exploring Kampala.

It was the capital, largest city, and primary commercial and education center of Uganda. Its many roads knit the country together, making the city a natural administrative center. As Uganda's showpiece, it was full of spacious gardens, bustling trade, and had a cosmopolitan atmosphere.

Some of our old friends from Entebbe had also moved there. Though we found many places to go and play, we missed the botanical gardens and Lake Victoria.

I liked the Apollo Hotel. Fourteen stories high and built on a small hill, it was of one the tallest buildings I'd

ever seen. A group of us came across it one day as we were exploring different areas of Kampala. Neither Bina nor I had ever seen an elevator. Neither had our friends. We wondered how people managed to get to the top. When we stood close to the building and looked up at the top, our necks hurt.

"Come on," I said. "Let's have a look inside."

"They won't let us in," said one of our friends.

"Why not?" I demanded. "We will request that they let us see the inside."

"Okay," Bina replied. "We'll be very quiet, then maybe they won't kick us out."

Five of us entered the lobby. It was quiet, and much cooler than it had been outside. A lady stood behind the front desk talking to a couple. She didn't see us. We walked past exhibits of preserved animals.

"How do they preserve these live animals?" I asked.

"They inject them with tranquilizers," said Bina.

As we approached the elevator its doors opened, and we stepped in. Nothing happened.

"You need to press the buttons," said one of our friends. When we started pressing different buttons, one girl stopped us. "Look, this one says top floor," she said. She pressed it firmly. The elevator started upward.

This was fun. In no time we reached the top. The door opened. We walked to the railings and realized this was where we could see the whole city.

"Come look over here," said Bina. "There is Kampala road. Where is our house?"

"Somewhere over there," I said, pointing. From that height the people and streets seemed so small.

From the other side we could see the swimming pool area down below. We tried to keep ourselves quiet as we watched the beautiful ladies in their bikinis, sipping drinks by the pool.

I pointed at a big black man. "Look," I said. "There's Idi Amin."

"Where?"

"I can't see him."

"There in the pool," I said.

A man who looked like Idi Amin stood in the pool with a young girl on one side and was surrounded by few other white and native women. When we'd all convinced ourselves that he was Idi Amin, we got scared, and ran towards the elevator. We pressed the button, but it seemed like hours. Our nervous impatience grew. Finally we heard the pulley sound. The door opened. We ran inside the elevator and started pressing all the buttons.

"This one," said Bina, pressing the button for the ground floor. Downstairs the woman at the front desk stared at us as we ran from the hotel as fast as we could.

The man we'd seen might have been Amin. We later heard rumors that he often came to that hotel to relax by the pool. We never returned.

CHAPTER 15

We were children, and felt little concern about what was going on in the government, but it was hard not to notice Idi Amin. Each day he would appear before microphones and cameras, telling the world how he would make Uganda a better place. Sometimes he appeared by himself. Other times he'd bring one of his wives, or a favored son.

We'd grown up assuming our country was safe. Now we were aware that it wasn't. Young African boys were harassing Indians like us. Mum heard a story about an African man who, in the middle of a busy bazaar, started cutting Indian peoples' arms. He hadn't been caught, and no one knew who he was. After that our parents didn't let us go out after sunset.

If we were going to the temple, or any other distant place, we were supposed to travel in a group.

Bina and I were teenagers now, and our free-time activities reflected that. We spent time adding and altering the designs of saris, colorfully threading them with pearls. We did this on weekends and during school vacations.

On Sundays, after finishing our household work, we walked on the main road to Kampala with our new friends. This road was packed with young Indian couples dressed in their best traditional clothing. The local street vendors lined both sides of the road, selling roasted corn, cassava fries and unripe mangoes sprinkled with lemon salt and red chili powder. Yummy.

Mum had little time for visiting new people. Instead they came over once a week to chitchat. Kantaben Joshi, a short chubby, warm-hearted woman with a friendly smile, visited every other Tuesday afternoon. Her sari couldn't hide her sagging waist. She spoke very slowly, and took deep breaths between speeches.

One Monday afternoon we were surprised to see Kantamashi at our house.*

---

* ben added to Indian women's name is a form of addressing

* mashi added to Indian women's name is a form of addressing by children to elderly women.

"Why is she here?" I whispered to Mum.

"Don't ask any questions," Mum commanded. "Go make chai."

I made an unpleasant face, pulled out the primus stove from underneath the shelves, and put a water pot on. While adding loose tea and chai masala, I listened to hear whatever I could.

"For the last few years, we are having a lot of obstacles in our entire family," Kantamashi told Mum. "According to the readings from our Brahman, our ancestors are caught up in hell. We need to pay homage to them. I've come to invite you and your family for a thirteen-day pritru puja and dinner. Saturday the 10th is Surya Grahan [new moon]. It's a great day to start. The day before the last day is Devshayani Ekadashi which falls on Saturday the 22nd. We've learned that these are auspicious days to perform the rituals. My husband and I will fast on the first and last days so that we do not leave anything undone. We've been told that, if we perform these sacred rituals correctly, our ancestors will be freed and will achieve heavenly moksha. Then they will bless us. We have invited friends and families. We will have plenty of food offerings.

"Because the government is so unstable, my husband and I have chosen to perform this ritual in July, instead of waiting until October, the month of Ashwin, which is more auspicious for these kinds of rituals."

Mum understood what Kantamashi was saying. She and her husband would be vocalizing certain mantras to invite the spirits of the ancestors who'd been passed over. They would then ask these spirits how their request could be fulfilled.

This happens when a certain spirit enters into a human body. The one who volunteers is usually a family member. The family asks who this spirit is, and what his or her wish is. Once this is clear, the family member who's performing the ceremony does whatever is necessary to satisfy the spirits on the 13th day. The requests are usually non-material tasks. Our family followed those kinds of traditions. Once a year Papa threw food on the roof to feed the crows. He always said it was to satisfy our ancestors.

"You must be sure to come," Kantamashi said.

"We definitely will," said Mum. "What time? And where is it?"

"It will be held at our Lohana Community Hall from 6 to 8 in the evening. The last day, we will be having an extended ceremony."

I was happy to hear this and made the tea stronger and more sugary than usual. I knew Kanta Aunty loved strong tea.

She saw what I was doing, and as she took the teacup from the serving plate she said, "Mila, one day, you will be a good wife."

I thought, *What nonsense is she is talking about!*

After she left, my siblings and I asked Mum about the event Kantamashi had been describing.

"Instead of all these questions, get your dresses ready," she said. "Look at what you have. Which dresses need to be fixed?"

We took our clothing from the suitcase, and began the task of readying ourselves for this mysterious event.

We counted days, marking the calendar until the day arrived. That day we came from school, had tea, cleaned ourselves, then put on our favorite dresses. Mum wore her beautiful sari, Papa was okay with a clean shirt and trousers.

"Come everyone, let's go," said Papa. "We don't want to be late on the first day."

We walked a little more than a mile. When we got there they let us play hide-and-seek in the garden with the other children until seven, when the food was served. We were too young to understand what was happening, so, though we went there all thirteen days, we attended only a few of the actual rituals. What impressed me was the Brahman's performance of the mantras. As he did this, he invited an ancestor's spirit to enter a young boy. The boy went into a trance, and he spoke in a woman's voice.

My sisters and I had our suspicions. We began to ask who this woman was, and what she wanted. The family member performing the ceremony recognized one of the family's ancestors. The family kept their promise and did what was asked after the ceremony. They gave the boy water, bringing him back to the real world.

The last day, we arrived early. As usual, we children played hide-and-seek in the front yard. It was a hot day. With the sun low in the western sky, three young black men sat in the middle of the nicely trimmed grass. Silent and unsmiling, they gazed towards the road. I watched them, wondering: *Don't they have to go home?*

Finally we went in for dinner. It was the last day, so it really was a feast this time. Mum and our aunty helped with the cooking. I told the boys serving dinner about the three men outside, but they ignored me.

After dinner, we waited for our parents in the kitchen. They were saying their goodbyes to our host. Most of the guests had left. The only ones left were the organizers and their families. It was already ten pm. "Let's go," we heard Papa say to Mum.

Our host told Papa, "I am honored you and your family came, and I'm happy the ceremony was so successful. Let me give you a lift home."

"Oh no," Papa said. "You should be tired. I don't want to give you any trouble. You still have a lot to do."

Mum, weary, and holding the sleeping Jaimini, insisted that Papa accept the lift. "It's too dangerous, walking by ourselves at this hour," she reminded him. Papa agreed.

Outside it was too dark to see anyone. Our host, uncle Kanubhai* told us to wait at the entrance while he went to the parking lot to get his Mercedes car. In the cold of the evening I saw the three men still sitting on the same spot. They hadn't moved. I was about to tell Mum when uncle Kanubhai pulled his car in close. Papa got in the front seat with Donna on his lap. At Mum's direction, we climbed into the backseat from the other side. Kevin and I sat in the middle while Bina sat near the door.

"Look at these leather seats," said Kevin. He wanted to see how uncle Kanubhai drove this car. We stared at all the buttons and knobs on the dashboard as Mum started getting into the back seat next to me. She was moving slowly, holding Jaimini in her arms. Uncle Kanubhai started the engine.

Mum was only half inside the car when suddenly these three men approached with fango(a club-like tool with a sharp blade). One came up on the driver's side, the other two on Papa's side. In Swahili they chanted: "Toka!

---

* 'Uncle' is a form in which children address all elderly Indian men.

Toka!" They were telling us to get out.

"Run, run," Mum cried. Still holding Jamini, Mum ran into the building. Leaving the motor running, Uncle Kanubhai got out. He ran toward the hall, followed by Papa and Donna. Papa kept shouting that we must run.

Bina, who was closer to the window, got out easily. Kevin and I were trapped in the middle seat. There was not much time to do anything as the three men climbed in, and drove the car away. I slid myself towards the door, then gripped the handle, waiting for an opportunity to jump.

The car slowed before turning onto the main road. Grabbing hold of my little brother's hand, I quickly opened the door and jumped out. As the car shifted gears, Kevin's hand slipped from mine. I hit the ground, scratching my arms and legs. I got up and ran towards the kitchen shouting for help. I shouted myself hoarse. Once inside, I hid underneath the dining table.

Mum saw me from the hallway. "Where is Kevin?"

"He is in the car," I said. "I tried to pull him out with me, but his hands slipped from mine."

Mum cried out, "God save my son!" People gathered to comfort her.

Not knowing what to do, Papa went out, calling for help. In response to his shouts some young boys picked up whatever they could find—rolling pins, sticks and so forth—and ran behind the car. Papa ran then stopped. Unable to catch up with the boys, he came back to the stairs and waited.

Half an hour later Papa saw some of the boys walking back. One carried Kevin on his shoulders. Papa ran to them and took Kevin.

"Papa, I was afraid," said Kevin. "I rolled from one side

to the other. I tried to open the door but it was too tight."

One of the boys told Papa, "Those men were not professional. They only came to steal the car."

"How did you catch them?" Papa asked.

"They did not know how to drive the car properly. They were going too slowly when the driver looked back at us. He accidentally swerved and hit a light pole. One ran, but the other two were still in the car. They had minor injuries. While my friends beat the men with sticks and kicked them, I made sure Kevin was safe, taking him from the back seat. We left the thieves on the road, unable to move."

The front of the car was damaged. The rest of the boys pushed it back to the entrance of the clubhouse. Uncle Kanubhai's older brother Uncle Vijaybhai gave us a ride home. We finally got back after midnight.

CHAPTER 16

One August day Papa rushed home from school and went straight into his room to listen to the news on the radio. He was so distracted by it that he didn't touch the tea Mum brought him.

"I will drink it later," he said.

Mum sat down next to him and listened. It was Amin. He was announcing that all those whose families had originally come from Asia must leave Uganda in the next 90 days. We could not take money, and we would be limited to 30 kilograms of baggage per person.

General Amin said that we were bloodsuckers. He claimed we were exploiting native Ugandans, while keeping a stranglehold on the economy. He ignored the fact that our industry and entrepreneurial efforts had made Uganda's economy stronger than it would have been otherwise.

Indians controlled the majority of businesses: such as factories, sugar cane plantations, tea estates, agriculture, construction, textiles and cotton gins. We were the backbone of Uganda's economy. Amin claimed that we'd refused to integrate with the black community. But we were a minority, unpopular among the native Ugandans, who resented our success. Our departure would signal the downfall of Uganda's economy.

Some Asians thought this must be a joke. The British would intervene, negotiating a settlement, or Amin would cave in, or be overthrown. But Amin was stubborn. He wouldn't cave, and it would be years before someone found the strength to subdue him. His ultimatum was serious. We had to go.

It was the next day's headline. Amin had ordered Israelis, British, Europeans and non-citizen Asians to leave within 90 days. He said he would exempt certain professionals, such as lawyers, doctors, and teachers. Anyone else who remained would be imprisoned or executed. Most of the Asians were Gujarati Indians and Pakistanis. We'd lived in this country for decades. We were second, third and fourth generation Ugandan residents. This was the only home we knew.

Amin soon amended his order, applying it to all Asian residents. Any of us who stayed would face prison. Britain's government wanted to know where these people would go. Of Uganda's 80,000 non-Ugandan Asians, over half were British passport holders. What would Britain do?

Britain's right-wing MPs warned that letting more Ugandan Asians into the UK could raise racial tensions. They urged that these people be forced to go elsewhere. They claimed we had no British ties, so the place for us should be India.

This had negative repercussions for native Ugandans. Many had jobs in Asian-owned businesses or households. They would now be jobless. Some people of Asian descent were citizens of Uganda. They would have to stay, and watch as many of their friends and family fled. Amin and his supporters saw all of us as foreigners, but we'd been born in Uganda. This was our home, and we loved it.

In Kampala, Asians flooded into the temporary Canadian immigration office. Those with British passports went to the British emergency processing office, seeking entry permits, but a welcome in the British Isles was far from guaranteed. In the English city of Leicester, advertisements warned Indians to stay away. They would not find jobs or housing there, the ads said. If Amin didn't want us, neither did anyone else.

CHAPTER 17

Originally Amin was regarded as a nationalist. His popularity increased when he got rid of Obote's secret police, freed political prisoners, and told Ugandans he would hand power back to his people. Uganda is for black people only, he roared But he did not consider people like us to be Ugandan. We were Asians and "foreigners" to him.

Many people said we should leave. Natubhai Patel and his family friend, Mr.Rameshbhai Shah, had established several successful businesses in Uganda. Both of them were devastated by Amin's policy. Their homes were ransacked. Natubhai said we should leave for our own safety. Many others lived the same story: businesses built over decades were now Africanized and given to Amin's cohorts. These businesses were plundered and ruined in a matter of weeks. Amin walked the streets of Kampala, acting as if he was the great black power of the African continent.

Papa worried for his family, but tried to stay cool. He had no intention of going back to India.

Mum panicked, often putting both her hands to the sides of her head as she squatted on the floor. "What shall we do?" she cried. "Where will I go with all these children?"

Losing patience, Papa would raise his voice. "I can't think if you keep on bothering me. I wish I had enough savings to buy our family tickets to India, but I don't. What shall I do?"

"What about our girls?" Mum demanded. "We keep hearing of these young girls being kidnapped and raped by soldiers."

"Nothing is going to happen," said Papa, trying to believe his own words. "We are not the only ones. There are thousands out there in the same situation. We will find a way."

One by one, the wealthier Indians fled, leaving their investments, businesses and estates behind. We were becoming a persecuted, powerless minority: harassed, threatened and with little real hope. It happened to us on the streets and on the walk to school, especially on the bus. One morning on our way to school, a local boy kept making faces at us. We tried not to look at him. He edged toward us and tried to touch my face. I slapped his hands and stared at him, as I snapped: "Don't touch me."

"Didn't you hear what Idi Amin said?" he asked, laughing at me.

I told our teacher, Miss Manjulaben, about it, but all she could say was, "Mila, you have to ignore it. Don't look at them or talk to them. I had an incident last week in my driveway. Luckily our dog, Moti, came barking, and the man ran away."

As the days passed, there were fewer and fewer of us. Indians and Pakistanis were leaving, just as Amin had ordered them to. Within a month only a few of us were left.

Students from the Langi and Acholi tribes were just as scared as we were. They had no other nation where they'd be welcome. Their only option was to flee to neighboring Kenya, and Kenya was closing its doors to them.

In school we weren't getting any more lessons. Instead we spent our time singing songs, playing board games, or telling stories to each other. Every day the students had new stories of disappearances, atrocities and deaths: young boys and girls who were forcefully taken away from their homes. Boys were recruited for training on the outskirts of Kampala, and girls were being raped, abused and many times killed, if they tried to escape.

In late August a boy named Bambino told us how his uncle, Mr. Abasi, arrived early one afternoon with three missionaries, two nuns and a priest named John.

Mr Abasi rushed into his house, found his wife, Abwot in the kitchen. She had their two-year-old daughter wrapped at her back as she began preparations for the evening meal.

She turned to him, surprised. "Why are you home so early?" she asked. "And why are you in such a panic?" Glancing outside at the missionaries, she inquired, "Abasi, who are those people? Why are they in our car?"

"I am on Idi Amin's hit list," said Mr. Abasi. "Pack warm clothes, food and drinks. We need to get out of Uganda right now." Mr. Abasi took off his policeman's uniform and put on formal clothing.

"Where shall we go?" Abwot asked.

"We must at least try to get to Kenya."

"What about my parents?" she asked. "Can we take them too?"

"No," he replied. "It's too risky to go to your parents' house. While trying to free a friend, your father killed one of Amin's men. He was captured yesterday. Amin's men are going to every village. They are killing innocent men and burning their homes."

Abasi went outside and pulled the car near the backdoor of their house. They loaded it up with blankets, food baskets, and water. Abwot sat in back holding her baby girl in her lap, their sons, 14 and 5, sat on both sides of her. The nuns were crammed in by the windows, and John, the priest, sat next to Mr. Abasi. They left their living room and kitchen lights on so people would think they were home. As they drove off, Abwot took one last look at their lovely house. They left it all behind.

They were going to Kisumu. The route was a long and rough one, often off the highway. They wanted to avoid any military personnel. Mr. Abasi was hoping to get to the border after midnight. He and the priest both took turns driving. Both the nuns entertained the boys, allowing their mother time to relax.

By sunset they still hadn't gone half the distance. When John asked Mr. Abasi to take a break, he pulled the car onto a small dirt road. The priest took the wheel, and they went on. Now it got darker. There were hardly any other cars on the Kisumu-Busia road, and the only noise was that of the car and its engine. Everyone in the car was asleep except John.

John was tired, but that didn't matter; he had to keep on driving. By two-thirty in the morning they were nearing the border. The priest stopped near a farm.

"Abasi, wake up!" called the priest.

They refreshed themselves with food and drink, and stretched their legs, then Abasi took the wheel for the second time.

"It is good the children are asleep," said John, looking back at the blanket covering the children and their mother. The two nuns had also spread their wide skirts over the children. The men in front assumed the nuns were sleeping.

Abasi pulled the car back on the road. He drove slowly, avoiding any excess noise. Then they reached the border where three soldiers sat on a wooden bench outside the post. The soldiers held their rifles straight as if they were going to shoot in the air. They stopped the carload of refugees.

One soldier, chewing a toothpick, pointed ahead into the darkness. "The road is blocked," he said, standing up and approaching Mr. Abasi on the driver's side. One of the other soldiers peered through the car windows on the passenger side to see who might be there. It was too dark to see much of anything. The third soldier remained seated, his rifle handy. Empty bottles of whiskey lay on the ground next to his foot. He was drunk.

"Where are you taking all these people?" asked the soldier with the toothpick.

Mr. Abasi replied in Swahili, "Ndugu zangu, I ni dereva wa kawaida kuchukua wamisionari hawa Kisumu kutembelea wamishenari marafiki zao." He was saying that he was just an ordinary driver taking the missionaries to Kisumu to visit their missionary friends.

"Show me your papers," said the one in command.

The priest and the nuns handed over their passports.

"Aha," said the soldier. "People of God, tourists to Kenya." Everyone in the car got quiet. He looked again at Mr. Abasi. "Where are your papers?" he shouted.

Abasi searched his pocket in vain, wondering what to do.

The soldier ran out of patience, and put his rifle barrel against Abasi's neck. "You get out."

At that moment John handed a bottle of whiskey and a box of Marlboro cigarettes to the one standing on the passenger side. The soldier snatched these, and went forward, holding his prizes to the light. "Oh! Johnny Walker," he said, opening the bottle.

He was about to drink when the commander shot into the air. "You are not drinking it now!" the man said. "We have not finished with their papers." He snatched the bottle from the other soldier's hands.

Frightened by the gunshot, Abasi knew it was the end. If he did not act, they would all be killed. This was his only chance. While the two soldiers argued over the whiskey, Abasi looked at John. Suddenly Abasi started the engine and drove full speed, knocking down two wooden signs. The soldier threw the bottle, then both of them started shooting. One of the nuns took a bullet to her shoulder.

Abasi drove nonstop for the next few kilometers. He finally stopped at the Kenyan border. The Kenyan government had relaxed the rules about passengers entering from Uganda. The guards didn't send them back. The injured nun was taken to the hospital. John and the other nun went with her. Abasi and his family drove further into Kenya. With every kilometer they felt safer. Mr. Abasi knew that he was one of the luckiest ones.

In our class everyone clapped their hands, applauding Bambino's story.

"How did you hear this story?" Miss Manjulaben asked.

"We got a phone call from my uncle," said Bambino. "We were glad he made it."

Then another student named Arti told us how an Indian family from her cousin's town had been getting ready to leave Uganda when Amin's men attacked their home. Luckily this family escaped with their lives.

One classmate spoke of a young Indian couple traveling from Gulu to Kampala. Drunken soldiers attacked and robbed them, then tied the man to a tree and raped his wife right in front of him. "Please!" he cried. "Don't do this. Let her go! Take everything we have!" His pleas were worse than useless; the more he cried, the more the soldiers taunted him by torturing his wife. They left her there to die, and chopped off the husband's head. A passing traveler saw the dying woman, helped her, and eventually she was reunited with her family in Kampala.

"This is very sad," said Miss Manjulaben. "Let's pray for everyone to be safe." We prayed for a few minutes, then got out of our last class earlier than usual.

Amin ordered his soldiers to kill all supporters of former President Obote. They did the work well, so he soon set them loose on any other groups he regarded as enemies. This could be anyone. Those who had ethnic, political or business reasons to oppose his regime were under threat of death. Amin ordered murders by using euphemisms that amounted to a code. One of his favorite code phrases was: "Give him the VIP treatment." This meant the victim was to be tortured until he died.

Whatever the means of killing, Amin meant to throw all his enemies to the crocodiles.

Life in Uganda had once been like paradise, but now every day dawned with a new threat. Soldiers were shooting innocents just to show their power, and when the troops felt they had any justification at all, they performed massacres. They slaughtered most of the Acholi and Langi officers right in their army barracks. Those tribes were among the first to suffer from Amin's wrath. For the rest of Uganda, the nightmare was only beginning!

As Amin consolidated his power, his other personality emerged. Gone was the charming dancer and his pretty speeches. This Amin was a merciless, unpredictable, cunning liar. In the coming months and years he would personally order the execution of the Anglican archbishop of Uganda, the nation's chief justice, the chancellor of Makerere College, the governor of the Bank of Uganda, and several of his own parliamentary ministers.

Eventually Amin's forces would be responsible for between 100,000 and 500,000 deaths. Most were ordinary citizens. In some cases entire villages were wiped out. The Nile River was the receptacle for so many corpses that they clogged the intake ducts at a nearby dam until workers fished them out.

Bina and I heard so many of these stories that we soon told our parents we didn't want to go to school anymore. Taking a bus all that way was just too risky. Papa had to think hard on that one. He had an educator's reverence for the classroom, and he never could've imagined allowing us to stay home. Yet he recognized the dangers, and finally gave his reluctant approval. It was a sad day.

Night and day, we were living in despair and fear. Fear that at anytime someone would come loot or kill us. The soldiers watched the streets and main roads like hawks, carrying machine guns to shoot anytime they wanted to.

CHAPTER 18

One of Papa's old acquaintances from the town of Kabale started showing up at our house every afternoon. The first time he arrived he said he was there to see Papa. He was a short, chubby man who never smiled and didn't say much. He wore his trousers tied high with a thin belt around his big fat stomach. He sat on a bench with his legs wide open, drinking tea from the saucer. His swallows made a big gulping sound.

He made Mum feel uncomfortable. She had no idea what to talk to him about. He irritated Bina and me by commanding us to make extra tea for him.

When this became too much, Bina asked: "How can we get rid of him? Can you figure some way to do that, Mila?"

We would've liked to simply tell him he wasn't welcome, but our polite upbringing wouldn't allow us to do this.

Papa was surprised to see this man. "Look who is here. Chimanbhai, what made you come all the way to Kampala?"

"I came to ask that you let me and my family stay here with you for one week," he said. "In ten days we are leaving for India."

"I need to ask my wife," said Papa.

Mum didn't like the idea. "There are already seven of us," she protested. "There are no extra rooms. Where will all of them sleep?"

Uncle Chimanbhai didn't give up. He continued asking Papa, and Papa sympathized with him. That evening at home, when the subject came up again, Mum and Papa had a big argument.

"We will manage," said Papa. "It's only a matter of one week."

Mum argued, but Papa somehow convinced her. "It's fine," she said, "as long as they don't bother me and our children."

The next day Bina and I found that we had to get out of our bedroom.

"Where are we going to sleep?" Bina asked.

"All of you will sleep in the living room," said Mum.

That was just the beginning. On Wednesday morning, a van arrived fully loaded with household items, three misbehaved children and two elders.

"If they're going to India, why have they brought so much stuff?" I asked. I didn't get an answer.

They somehow managed to get everything into our small bedroom. They had only a small place left for sleeping and cooking. All three children were boys, ages 9, 7 and 2. From the start they got on our nerves: running, fighting, and mistreating our things.

When ten days had passed, Bina asked when we would get our room back.

"I don't know," Mum said. "These people have not said anything to Papa yet. They are still shopping for daily groceries, and, as of today, they have not packed anything."

Finally Mum told Papa to make them leave. "The agreement was for one week only," she reminded him. "Their boys are constantly disturbing our daughters."

Papa didn't have the courage to tell uncle Chimanbhai, but Mum kept at him. A month passed.

One day Papa took uncle Chimanbhai for a walk. "Our house is overcrowded," he told his friend politely. "It would be better if you and your family find another place. You said this would only be for ten days, but it's been a month already. When are you going to leave for India?"

"I am looking to get a better deal," Uncle Chimanbhai said.

"But there are no better deals now," said Papa.

"Please let me stay for a little longer," Uncle Chimanbhai begged.

Papa gave in and allowed it.

This made Mum mad. "You do not listen to me," she told Papa. "I told you not to let them stay in the first place. I would like to help them but they are not honest."

Torn between his wife and friend, Papa was helpless. It wasn't until two months had passed that uncle Chimanbhai and his family left for India, leaving most of their possessions behind. Their tickets had finally been confirmed

In October, when the first day of Navaratri festival arrived, there was no festival. Instead of nine days of dancing, evening discussions took place at the temple.

The day after Navarati was Dussehra, the day when we observe that no matter how strong evil may seem, good always prevails. That day we arose early, made breakfast for the family, cleaned the house, cooked and took care of the laundry. Doing laundry was the most fun. We washed our clothes by hand, enjoying the occasional spray of cold water. Rolling bed sheets at both ends, we wrung them out. We dried the clothes on a line strung up on the roof.

Mum made various foods, offering them to the gods, as we prayed for protection and safety.

Papa was still teaching at a nearby school. There he talked to other Asian families, encouraging them. They did the same for him.

On the afternoon of Dussehra, after Papa had returned to school, we were scrubbing the kitchen floor. Mum was in her room resting. Suddenly we heard a knock on the front door.

"Go see who it is, Mila," Bina said.

I peered out through the curtain. When I recognized our visitor I shouted: "Mum! It's Uncle Krishnakant." I was so happy to see him. I liked Uncle* Krishnakant. He always made me laugh. I opened the door.

"Why are you not in school?" he asked, putting his hand on my head. "Go make us a nice cup of tea."

Quickly I mentioned the troubles we'd seen and heard about at school, and the harassment we received on the bus. As I heard Mum stirring, I ran into the kitchen and brought back tea for both of them.

Uncle Krishnakant was a childhood friend of Papa's. He was about six feet, with an athletic body. He weighed about 220 pounds. He had acne scars all over his face, and wore tinted glasses. He was always dressed in nice pants and a shirt he never tucked into his trousers. He was intelligent, good-hearted and caring. With his partner Ram, he owned a successful transport company.

He had some storage space beneath our apartment, and now and then he dropped by to store something, or take something out. Whenever he did that he visited us.

Mum came out from her bedroom, and greeted Krishnakant with her tired, worried face.

"What's going on?" he asked Mum.

"I am worried about the girls," she said. "They don't want to go to school anymore, and I do not know what to do about it."

Uncle Krishnakant and Mum talked, as Bina and I sat on the floor listening.

"Uncle," I said, "next time you go to Arua, do take me with you. It is fun sitting on the ferry."

"I don't go to Arua anymore," he said, sipping his tea.

"Why?" I asked.

Before he could reply, the front door opened and Papa entered with Donna and Kevin. Bina went to the kitchen to make fresh tea for Papa.

Hey, you, Krishnakant! Papa greeted him. "What brings you here?"

"Sit down," Uncle Krishnakant said. "I have something to tell you."

Papa sat next to him; Bina gave Papa his tea, and went back to the kitchen to warm milk for Donna and Kevin. Mum stood up and went to her room, leaving these friends to their talk.

***

"I am leaving for England, this coming Friday with my family," Uncle Krishnakant told Papa. "What are your plans?"

"I have no plans," said Papa. "I am staying here in Uganda. My only worry is for my family. It has become too dangerous for the girls to go out."

"Babu," said Uncle Krishnakant. "all of you must get out of Uganda. It is too risky for foreigners to stay. Think of your family. How would you feel if something happened to these girls?" He put his hand on my head again. "If you want you stay, that's fine, but let your family go back to India. At least they will be safe over there."

"Yes," Papa agreed. "I now realize that. I wish I had saved some money. The tickets have become very expensive. Even though I want so much to send them to India, I could not afford to buy six tickets. Besides, I will have to give them something extra to start their lives over there. You know how it is in India."

Uncle Krishnakant said: "I will provide you with money to buy the tickets. They will stay in our house over there. I will send a message to my mother in India to look after them in case they need anything. But I have one request. Our parrot, Jade, is 85 years old. We do not want to take him to the cold country. I will appreciate if you take him to India and give him to my mother."

As I came in with a fresh cup of tea for my uncle, I said, "Wow a parrot! Does he speak?"

"Yes," my uncle replied. "He speaks a lot, and he repeats what you say. So Mila, you need to watch what you say." He laughed. After finishing his tea, he stood up and tapped me gently on my head with his thick hands. "The tea was delicious," he said. "Did you prepare it?"

"Yes, I made the second cup," I said with a smile.

"I must go," he said as he moved towards the door.

"Saita," Papa called, addressing Mum. "Krishnakant is leaving."

Mum came out of her bedroom.

"Krishnakant is leaving for England with his family," Papa told her.

"Oh? When?" she asked feeling sad.

"This Friday."

"I am glad for you. Please, stay for dinner."

"No," said my uncle. "I ate a lot of the goodies you made. I am already full."

"Then come for lunch with your family before you leave," Mum suggested.

"It is nice of you, but we have so much to do before we go," he said.

Papa escorted him to the door and thanked him.

After he left, Papa told Mum, "Krishnakant is going to give us money for the tickets. I want you to take the children to India."

"What about you?" she asked.

"I will stay here in Uganda," said Papa.

"But it's not safe," said Mum. "We must all travel together and start our new life in India."

"I left India not intending to go back," said Papa. "You should not worry. I will be okay. There are many men like me. No harm will come to me. You take care of the children."

The next day all of us were having an afternoon nap. Mum and Papa were in their room, and we children were playing in the living room. The doorbell rang. When Mum opened the door there was a tall, thin, friendly-looking man with a round face. This was uncle Ram. Uncle Ram was uncle Krishnakant's business partner, but they seemed more like brothers. They even lived together with their wives and their children.

"Oh, hello Rambhai," Mum said. "How are you doing? It is always nice to see you. Have a seat."

Uncle Ram held a thick plastic carrier bag in one hand and a cage with a parrot in the other. He put the cage on the ground and handed a bag tied with a big rubber band to Mum. "Here," he said. "This is for your tickets to India, and some extra for on the way."

Mum opened the bag, looked in and her eyes grew big. She had never seen so much cash. She called Papa: "Come look at what's here." She turned to uncle Ram. "You saved our lives, Rambhai."

"Put it somewhere safe," he said.

A lot of homes were being robbed in the middle of the day, so this was good advice. Mum dumped the bag in the big bin full of rice.

After washing his face, Papa came in and sat next to uncle Ram.

"I wish you could stay for dinner," Mum said to our guest.

Uncle Ram motioned to the cage. "Here is our dear Jade, and this is his food."

Bina, always an animal lover, came in and sat down next to the cage. I did the same. "Oh, look how pretty he is," said Bina.

"Oh, look how pretty he is," said Jade the parrot.

"He speaks," I said. We all laughed.

"You have to be careful," said uncle Ram. "He will repeat what you say, sometimes even after a few days."

We sat in a circle around the cage. The parrot had grey feathers, a black beak, and a beautiful cherry red tail.

"He is 85 years old," said uncle Ram. "Make sure you take enough food to last the long journey."

Jade whistled.

"Wow! He talks and he whistles," I said.

Mum had us make tea, while she rubbed special oil on uncle Ram's neck. He had eczema on his neck, so each time he came over Mum rubbed it with oil, easing his pain. After having tea, he departed, leaving the parrot with us.

The following Saturday was a very busy day. Mum got up early in the morning and prepared to cook. It was a special dish. We prepared small roti's filled with sweetened chana paste and sprinkled with ghee on the top, two kinds of vegetable dish, soup and desert. I helped with that, while Bina finished the rest of the housework.

After breakfast Papa went to the travel office that was on Kampala road, to book our tickets. He came home sad.

"How did it go?" Mum asked.

"There are no seats available this week," Papa said. "The agent told me to come next Wednesday. If I am lucky, he could find a place by the last week of October. There are places available for two and four, but not for six people together. You cannot travel sitting separately."

"The agencies are open seven days a week, so you must keep going to the agency every day," said Mum. "We must get on that train before the deadline."

Papa had invited his best childhood friend, Uncle Jeetu, and his wife, Devimashi to lunch. They brought their two sons, 15 and 9. Uncle Jeetu and his family were leaving for India the next day.

This family arrived exactly at noon. All of us sat on the place mat, and the food was served. We began to eat.

"What are you taking with you?" Mum asked Devimashi.

"I packed some household items," Devimashi answered, "and some of our clothing. I have no idea how my boys will adjust to life in India. They've grown up here in such an easy, friendly environment." She took a deep breath, fighting off tears. Mum handed her a glass of water.

"It's okay," said Mum. "They will get used to it. You are lucky you got reservations. Babu is trying to get reservations for all six of us, but none are available for that many."

Uncle Jeetu looked at Papa. "How about you, Babu? You are not going?"

"He won't listen to me," Mum said. "Please, tell him to come with us. It is not safe anymore in Uganda. Every day, we are hearing of people disappearing and being murdered."

"That's true," said Devimashi. "You should not risk your life. You should leave too. Jeetu thought he would stay, and we got into a big argument. Finally he decided to come with us. Our boys are happy about that. We will live with his family in our village for a short while until we figure out which city we want to move to. Amit is at an age where he is ready for college."

Papa listened to all this, but made no comment.

After lunch, the adults chatted in the living room while Bina and I cleaned the kitchen. Mum told Bina to prepare tea. The boys stayed on the balcony.

"We should go," Uncle Jeetu finally said, standing up. "It is already three pm."

Mum offered everyone dried Fennel seeds (a tradition in every Hindu family to eat Fennel seeds after each meal for good digestion).

"We will come to the station tomorrow, and wish you a safe journey, said Papa. "God knows when we will see each other again."

From then on, every day at noon Bina took Jade's cage into the kitchen. There she fed the bird a piece of warm roti. Jade didn't like me at all. One day, as I tried to feed him a piece of carrot, he bit my finger. "Go away, go away," he said. He'd learned that one from Bina. Jade was intelligent.

Jade soon seemed like a part of our family. Mornings he called out: "Wake up, wake up. It's eight am. It's time to go to school."

At four in the afternoon he would call: "Matiya mogo tiya." He was asking someone named Matiya to cook cassava. It turned out that Matiya had been a boy working at uncle Krishnakant's house.

We couldn't roam around town anymore. We could only go to certain stores during daylight hours. In the evenings we hung around on the balcony.

One evening, not long after we'd received Jade, I stood on the balcony gazing at the quiet street. Everyone looked happy. All the businesses had closed for the day. Except for a few taxis waiting for the last passengers, I saw no one. Suddenly two Lorries approached. I dropped down on my knee and looked from behind the bars. Three young men were in the front of the first lorry. It rolled slowly down the street with something dripping out its side. It was red liquid. Then, as the lorry came closer, I saw a part of a body with its skin peeled off. The stench was horrible.

I felt my last meal rising up from my stomach. I held my breath, clenching my mouth shut. Both lorries were loaded with corpses. On one the cover had blown off in the wind. I stood up slowly. The lorry turned towards the corner. I threw up all over my dress. I was unable to stand.

Mum came to check the front door. "What you are doing out here this late?" she demanded. "Look at your dress. You made the balcony dirty."

Hearing Mum's voice, Papa came out. "What's going on?"

I told them what I'd seen.

"Don't you worry," Papa said. He helped me to the bathroom where I cleaned up. Mum filled a bucket with warm water and a few drops of Dettol, and washed the rest from the balcony.

CHAPTER 19

Later I heard Mum and Papa whispering in their bed.
"We need to do something," said Mum. "This cannot go on. After breakfast tomorrow, go again to the agencies. Insist that we must have tickets. We have only twelve days left before the deadline.'

Right after that she said, "I have no idea how life will be after we go. I am worried."

If Mum was worried, so was I. That night I had a fever. I stayed in bed for two days. Mum gave me hot milk with fever syrup and light food, such as gravy kichadi (rice cooked with lentils) with yogurt.

Papa tried the agencies again and again. He waited in the queue for hours, hoping to get the seats he needed. Most people got the bookings they wanted. Some did not.

After days of this, Papa got frustrated and sad. Mum's anxiety grew each time Papa came home empty-handed. She prayed harder.

Finally, after hard prayers, one evening in late October, Papa came home with a big smile. He looked at Mum and said, "Start packing. All of you are leaving in five days. I booked the tickets for October 31st. I paid full rate for six of you and half for the parrot."

At long last Mum felt better. She was so flustered, she didn't know what to pack. After having a good strong tea, she cooled down.

Papa and Mum sat talking in the kitchen for hours, while we children sat in our room. We were excited. We had great expectations of train travel and a voyage on a ship. We were going to a country unknown to us: India. We were going to see uncles, aunts and cousins we'd only heard of for the very first time. We'd never had any real cousins, uncles, aunts or grandmas nearby before. They'd been a distant thought across a wide ocean. We thought life in India would be good, growing up surrounded by a big family. Questions started storming our brains. How would it be to walk down the street and see nothing but brown-skinned people like ourselves? We were used to living among people of many colors, including a vast majority of black folks.

This was going to be an adventure.

***

The next day Mum set out every item we would take. Cluttering the living room with pots, pans and clothing, she separated items that must be checked with the transport people, and those we would carry with us.

Papa took off from school and went through the paperwork. He made sure our passports were valid, then wrote all the pertinent information we would need in a small address book. All day he listened to radio news reports, gauging whether it was safe to travel.

The Ugandan authorities allowed each traveler luggage weighing 30 kilograms. Between the six of us we could take 180 kilos out of Uganda. We couldn't take much money, but we didn't have much. We packed big, breakable items in with bed sheets, pillows, extra towels and the rest of the clothing. These fit in three small aluminum containers which we would check with the transport people. We poured rice and grains out so that we could use their containers. We packed two small suitcases with clothing and toilet items for the journey. We stuffed one big bag with homemade snacks, and a separate bag for parrot food and other parrot items.

While everyone was busy packing, Jaimini slipped out to the balcony. I noticed the front door standing open. I went out and looked down at the Sunday morning street. It was almost empty, except for a young man standing on the walkway. He had a candy in his hand, and seemed to be offering it to someone on the stairs. His dirty hair came to his shoulders, and his floppy trousers had probably never been washed. His shirt had a couple of broken buttons. He had the long dark features of an Indian.

I ran towards the stairs and saw Jaimini already halfway down. She teetered there, holding onto the railing, as she descended another step. She was staring at the candy. The young man pulled out a second candy, and I heard him urging Jaimini, "Step faster."

"Hey! What are you doing?" I shouted. "Are you trying to kidnap my baby sister?" At the sound of my scream, he ran away. I told Mum what happened. It was one more nightmare among many.

The next day, Mum, Bina and I went to say goodbye to our neighbors. When Mum knocked, nobody answered.

"Mum, they are not home," said Bina. "Let's go home."

"I will try again," said Mum, knocking harder this time. "Vidiyaben," she called our neighbor's name. "It's me. Saitaben."

One of Vidiyamashi's daughters peered out from behind a curtain. Finally the door opened.

"Sorry," said Vidiyamashi. "We are careful when opening the door. There's been so much looting. My friends' house was robbed last week. The thieves know the Indians have a lot of gold and other expensive items."

"I know how it is," said Mum as she walked in. "So how are things going with you, Vidiyaben?"

"Well, my eldest daughter Sita, who lives in Gulu, is here," Vidiyamashi said, introducing her daughter, who was holding her baby.

Sita greeted Mum. "I will make tea," she said, heading for the kitchen.

Mum and Vidiyamashi sat down at the dining table and starting sharing gossip.

"We are leaving for England this Thursday, the 28th," said Vidiyamashi. "I thank my dad. He got us British passports many years back. He saw what went on in Kenya in 1962, and felt that one never knows what might happen here. Yesterday, we went to the British consulate. There was a big crowd of people waiting to get approval to go to England. It took us the whole day. I have heard from friends that England has severe winters, and that it snows there. They say we will have to wear multiple layers of clothing just to stay warm. I've heard we will need pullovers, gloves, warm sock and boots, and that we must make sure we have our heads covered. I don't know how I will handle the cold with my back pain. I don't like wearing too many layers of clothing. It's like wrapping up in a cocoon.

"Sita came from Gulu two days ago with her husband and the baby. They bought a big house three years ago, but now they will have to leave everything behind. They are flying to India on the 2nd of next month." Vidyamashi's voice broke. Tears welled up in her eyes. "My daughter and I will be separated. We wished we could have applied for a British passport for her too. God knows when we will see each other again."

Sita came back with three cups of tea and some snacks. She sat next to Mum, while feeding her son a bottle of warm milk. Hearing her mother talking about her, Sita said, "We had to leave behind our beautiful big house, all the expensive furniture, our Mercedes, and most of all, our dear pet, Juno. We left with only five big suitcases. We gave the house keys and car keys to our maid." Now Sita started crying, and we all got emotional.

Mum blew her nose, then wiped away her tears. "My children and I are also leaving for India at end of this month," she told them. "My husband will be staying behind. I insisted that he come with us, but what can I do? He is stubborn."

A young man in his early 20s came in and sat at the table with us. He was pale and looked frightened.

"Why are you upset, Salish?" Vidyamashi asked him.

The boy hung his head.

"I will bring a glass of water and make fresh tea," said Sita.

"You sit," Vidyamashi told her. "I will call Dipika." Vidyamashi turned to Mum. "You see Saitaben, since Sita arrived, she is constantly on her feet helping me, doing this or doing that. This is how we Indians have trained our daughters. They never say 'no.' They do all that we ask, and more." She called her other daughter, Dipika. "Make tea for everybody, and bring a glass of water for Salish," she said, then she went on to explain to Mum, "Salish is our paying guest. He works at the airport."

After having some tea, Salish began his story. "At the airport I was stacking luggage when soldiers in tanks rolled towards a plane. Other workers and I hid amongst the luggage. When the soldiers surrounded the plane, one of the portals flew open and a man tried to flee. They caught him and threw him down on the runway. This man's wife and children were watching. One soldier said to the other, 'Take him to the police barracks and beat him up.' No one knows what happened to him or his family.

"After they left, I got scared. I wanted to come home. I didn't bother to take my things. I went into the restroom, changed my clothing, and walked to the parking lot. As I drove from the airport, I saw mutilated bodies hung like meat on hooks. My legs trembled, and I couldn't get my foot to press down on the accelerator. My heart grew hard like a stone. I couldn't move faster, and I still don't know how I made it home. I won't go to work anymore."

"Then what will you do?" asked Vidyamashi. "Though you have a decent job, all of us are leaving. Soon you will be all by yourself. Yet, with your Ugandan citizenship, you cannot go to any other countries."

"Don't worry about me." He got depressed and left for his room.

Mum stood up. "Thank you for the tea," she said. "I wish you and your family a safe journey. Bina, Mila let's go. We have a lot of work to do."

Vidyamashi thanked Mum for stopping by. "I wish you also a safe journey," she said, completing the sad farewell.

That night Mum stayed up late, making sure she had packed the necessary items. She was tired, but wanted to be certain we had what we needed. Papa tied the suitcases and metal containers with ropes, taping large destination addresses on each of them.

When we woke up the next morning, our house was nearly empty. It was October 31st, and we would be departing soon. We all sat down for our last supper with Papa. After supper, Donna and Kevin were put to bed, while Bina and I packed the kitchenware. We left a few pots and pans for Papa so he could do some light cooking and make tea. He also had an invitation from some remaining acquaintances to come have his lunch with them each day.

When the kitchen was done, Bina mopped the whole house. Papa and Mum checked the paperwork again. Our passports, birth certificates, and other important papers would be in Mum's purse at all times. From our bedroom, we could hear them whispering. We were too excited to sleep. We were going on the first long journey of our lives. How would life be for Papa without us? When we would see him again? We had to have faith that it would happen.

CHAPTER 20

The following day we left the only home we'd ever known for the last time. We were escaping three days before the deadline. This was when the big change hit me.

Bina and I got up at six and found Mum had already been up for over an hour. It seemed as if she hadn't slept at all. She packed our lunches and snacks, then left a large container of food items for Papa. She'd set aside just enough to feed us a small breakfast. She then washed herself and did her final check.

As we ate our breakfast, Papa told us stories of his childhood growing up in India. That's where he'd received his schooling. He told us of the two grandmothers we would see there, as well as uncles, aunties and cousins.

Listening to his stories of India, Donna made comical faces. Holding both hands together, she pretended to beg, "Please someone give me food. I have not eaten for many days." As Kevin began copying her, Bina and I laughed, but Papa got mad.

"Stop it, both of you," he said, standing up. "Where did you get these ideas?"

"From my classmate, Sandhia," said Donna. "She said we will see many beggars in Bombay, and that is how they beg." When she started doing it again, Papa stopped her.

"You must understand," he said, "Bombay has so many people, and not everyone can find work. This is true of every large city in the world. When they have nowhere to live, they end up on the street, and when they are hungry, they beg."

After breakfast, Bina handed me two thermoses and a bag. "Fill these with fresh tea and put them together in this snack bag," she said. "I must get Donna, Kevin and Jaimini ready."

Mum was still in her night sari, and her hair was loose. She put our passports and tickets into a compartment of her purse where she could pull them out without disturbing any other important papers. Papa locked all our traveling containers with a padlock. After breakfast I cleaned the kitchen. Donna and Kevin threw grain at each other, making a mess on the living room floor.

"Stop it," I shouted, catching them each by the neck. "We will miss our train. Take this broom and sweep it all up." Donna cried, and I realized I was clutching her hand far too tightly.

Mum was already tired, and could not take this anymore. She upset Donna, slapping her on both cheeks. "You do what your older sister says," she snapped.

Donna sat down in the corner and bawled.

"Let her cry," Mum ordered. "She will get over it soon. Make some fresh tea for us." I brought tea into the living room and served one to Papa.

"Leave it on the desk," he said.

I gave Mum a cup too.

Papa sipped his tea while checking our baggage. Bina got Jaimini ready. Jaimini was holding her adorable doll, and wouldn't give it up. By nine am all the luggage was ready. The only thing left to do was for each of us to put on our favorite outfits, then comb our hair. Mum put on her nice sari, combed her hair, then tied it in a ball and put a tilak on her forehead (a significant symbol for every married Hindu woman), using a special reddish powder called kamku. She was finally realizing that we were leaving Uganda for good. We were leaving our home, and most of our possessions. Worst of all, we were leaving Papa. How would he manage alone?

Mum carried these responsibilities for all of us, keeping her sadness to herself.

***

At ten-thirty a minivan and a taxi arrived. Two local men carried our luggage downstairs, loading the containers into the minivan, and tying our suitcases to the top of the taxi. Kevin and Papa went in the minivan. The rest of us took the taxi. Mum cautioned Papa to keep an eye on the luggage. They both knew that bags could easily get lost or stolen during an emotional departure like this one.

The minivan took off. After Bina and I had checked the house thoroughly, we girls took our place in the taxi. The driver started the engine.

"Stop," Mum commanded.

"What is it?" we asked.

Mum got out, went back in the house, then visited each room with a prayer on her lips. She came out looking sad, and began to cry. It was time to go.

It was a very hot day. As wind blew dust into the taxi, I felt this would be the last Ugandan soil on my skin. We were all sad, feeling the loss of our home, friends, school and mostly our papa. How life would be for papa was a question I kept asking.

The roads around the railway station were jammed with cars and taxis. It took ten minutes to reach the main entrance. We found Papa waiting at the gate with the tickets.

"Kevin," he said, "keep an eye on the luggage. I will go help your mum and sisters."

At the gate a friendly black ticket collector spoke of his sadness at seeing all the Indians leaving. As he checked our tickets, soldiers scrutinized everyone.

"All of you go stand in line over there," said Papa. He then followed a station employee and they checked our luggage.

The line was long. From the rear of the line we could see the controller's desk. Next to him stood a policeman who was checking that each person matched his or her passport photo. Once one's identity was confirmed, the policeman directed the person to go to the controller's desk.

The controller was a mean man in his 40s. He'd settled his 300 pounds onto a tiny chair that looked as if it might collapse under his weight. We prayed he would stamp our passports without finding any issues. Our worries were mostly for Jade the parrot. He wouldn't keep quiet. We worried that he would anger the controller, who might then refuse to let us go.

"Hujambo," the controller greeted Mum.

"Hujambo," she replied, handing over our tickets and passports. He glared at us. We stood up straight, not moving an inch. He looked at the cage the policeman was holding. That was where we had Jade.

At that moment Jade bit the policeman, who then let the cage fall on the controller's desk.

"Take this beast out of my sight," the controller shouted. He ground his teeth as he stamped our passports, and handed them back to Mum. I shivered as I realized there was no turning back.

We walked straight to the platform, where we waited for Papa.

"Look!" Kevin cried, pointing at the train. "Wow!"

The train was so long we couldn't count the carriages. It was a specially scheduled train for fleeing Indians. Many of us would be taking a train for the first time. We would be riding on rails laid by our ancestors at the cost of many lives. Those workers hadn't known that their descendants would be riding the same rails, fleeing the land of our birth. Our journey would take almost three days.

We children wondered what it would be like to sit on the train. I wondered from where tap water came and where the water went after flushing. Did it run down onto the railroad? These were my crazy thoughts as we waited anxiously for the train doors to open.

The station was full of sad people: some looking for acquaintances for company on their journey; some sat on their luggage; many said farewell to their loved ones.

Passengers rushed this way and that on the platform. The children were all excited. Parents said their goodbyes, as husbands told their wives to be careful. All the adults carefully guarded their children and their possessions.

It was noon. The hot sun was directly overhead, but none of us complained. We stood in the corner with

Papa as he told us about our luggage. "It's being checked in," he said. "Here's the receipt. You will need to show this in Bombay harbor to get the luggage back."

Mum put the receipt with our other important papers.

"Babu!" someone called from the crowd.

Papa looked back. "It's Jagdishbhai, with his wife Ashaben and children," he exclaimed, recognizing one of the teachers from his school. "So you booked your tickets ahead of us," said Papa.

"Yes," said Uncle Jagdishbhai. "I did not tell anyone because, even then I was not sure I was going. My mother is sick, and I did not want to leave her behind. In the end she insisted, and there was no other way."

"But who will take care of your Mum?" Papa asked.

"Our neighbors," he answered.

"Why is your husband not going with you?" Ashamashi asked Mum.

Mum told the story. "I am worried, but what can you do? I left snacks for Babu that should last six months."

Uncle Jagdishbhai offered us any help we might need on our journey.

"I am so glad you will accompany my family," said Papa. "It is always good to travel with someone we know. It's a very long journey and one never knows what one might need."

Finally, at fifteen minutes after noon the doors opened. We were anxious to get to our seats. We walked from one end of the train to the other, looking for our carriage. The first and second classes were in front, then we found the number five carriage.

"Go find our seats," said Mum. "I will be there soon."

We scrambled into our carriage. It was chaos. Men, women and children were pushing, pulling, and moving luggage around. People outside were shoving bags up to waiting hands at the windows. As we searched for our seat numbers, a chubby boy pushed me so hard that I almost fell on an older lady. I glared at him, but he didn't care.

Kevin rushed ahead, and cried out, "It's here."

Our bunks were near the end of the carriage. The bunks were lined up on each side of the aisle, facing each other. We had three reserved bunks, two facing each other and the third at our back facing the wall. From our seats we could see our parents on the platform. We took our seats after putting the two suitcases into the overhead compartment. We slid the rest of the bags underneath the seats. The seats were wooden, not very comfortable for a two-and-a-half-day trip. We would sleep and sit on the same seat. Like all passengers, we had to provide our own bedding.

It was a colonial-built train whose spacious first class had leather seats that folded out into sleepers. First class passengers were given crisp white linen and other luxuries, but there were fewer amenities during Amin's rule. I didn't see the second class facilities.

In our carriage Donna and Kevin each took the window seat. Mum and Jaimini would be on the same bunk with Kevin. I sat next to Donna. Bina took the back seat with Jade. The wooden sliding windows were big enough that we could stick our heads out.

When Mum arrived, she arranged the food, drinks and our carry-on bags so we could easily reach whatever we needed. We then went out for our final farewell to Papa. We hugged him and he looked at us sadly. He had no words, and held back his tears. We knew this would be the last time we would talk to him for some time. We lived in a time and place when long distance phone calls were extremely rare. For some while our only means of communication would be by telegram or letter. And who knew what would get through with Amin in power?

CHAPTER 21

At not quite an hour past noon the guard blew the first whistle. Smoke rose from the engine. We could smell the old rusty parts of the train.

"Mum, come!" we cried out. "The train is going to leave in five minutes. Mum! The doors will close!"

Mum cried as she separated herself from Papa.

Papa came to the train window where he took each of our hands, one-by-one, in his. "You will be safe," he told us. "Take care of each other. I will write, and reunite with all of you very soon." He didn't show his sadness, but we could feel it in the gravity of his words. At that moment I began to understand that women and men have different ways of crying. Men cry from their hearts, while women shed tears openly.

Deep down Papa was confident that he was doing the right thing. He was sending his family to a safer place, but he was staying in the place where we'd made our home. Uganda was where he'd seen his children born, and he hoped for a better day there. He would wait to see what happened. He had full faith in himself and knew in the depths of his heart that one day he would reunite with us.

At one pm the guard blew the third whistle. The door closed and the train took off. Now we were locked in for two-and-half days. We hoped that when we stepped off this train, we would be in a place that was safe.

The rhythmic motion of the train made me sleepy, and I nodded off. I was awakened by a baby crying, and I opened my eyes. We were passing through coffee plantations, then banana plantations. Mum remained silent, keeping her sadness to herself. It took her another half hour before she was willing to talk. We'd brought tea, and Mum felt better after she'd had a cup.

A man watched us from across the aisle. "Hello," he said in Gujarati. "I am Pravinbhai Khothari, and meet my wife, Neeru." He gestured to the woman sitting next to him. She was fair-skinned, and though she wore diamond earrings and a necklace, she seemed timid. Nevertheless she smiled at us.

"We are from Arua," said Uncle Pravinbhai. "Where are you all from?"

Mum greeted the couple, saying, "We are from Kampala, though we have family friends from Arua. Krisnakant Patel. Do you know them?"

"Everyone knows everyone in our small town," said uncle Pravinbhai. "Krishnakant and Rambhai are well known. They both are gentlemen. I had established a successful financial business there. Of course, I left everything behind."

"Where are your parents?" Mum asked.

Uncle Pravinbhai's voice grew sad. "My father was a doctor in Kampala," he said. "He was sent a package with a note ordering him to give high doses of medicine to one of his patients. My father refused. A week later both my parents were found burned to death in their car. Though I know nothing of India, my grandfather told stories about Rajkot and his extended family. Also, Neeru loves to watch Hindi movies, and I learned a lot from those.

"We are going to India for the very first time—the land of our ancestors. I have heard that it's a spiritual place. The historical temples are incredible. Neeru wants to see the Taj Mahal. I told her she would have to put that on her wish list. First I must start earning a living. We've brought just enough with us for our daily bread and living expenses."

"Do you have family in India?" Mum asked.

"Yes," said uncle Pravinbhai. "Distant relatives we've never had contact with before. We hope to connect with them. For a short time we will be staying at their place. Remembering my grandfather's stories of Rajkot and his extended family, I looked in his box of letters and found their address."

Mum took out pillows, blankets, and bed sheets, making our seats more comfortable, then prepared food. She put it in steel dishes we'd brought with us. This was before the days of disposable dishes and cutlery.

"Mum, did you bring Mango chutney?" asked Kevin. He loved mango pickles.

"Mila, it's in that bag," said Mum. "Make sure you don't pour the oil out while opening the bottle."

After having her tea, Mum laid down with Jaimini. After her long busy day, she fell asleep immediately.

I was curious about the landscape, and whether we were passing through the plantations we'd learned about in our geography lessons. I sat watching the scenery to see if it matched my knowledge. Suddenly, a cool breeze blew into our carriage.

"Wow! Mum, Bina! Look!" I called. We were crossing the River Nile. I knew we were in Jinja. We could see the Owen Falls Dam. Looking at the white froth of the water, and hearing it flow, reminded me of my school trip to Jinja when we'd seen the Coca Cola factory. We'd learned how the dam generated much of the electricity for Uganda and Kenya. From that trip I also knew that the Nile was the world's longest river, going all the way from here to northern Egypt, where it emptied into the Mediterranean Sea.

Mum woke up, glanced at the river, and went back to sleep.

It was very quiet on the train. Most of the elders and young children were resting. We passed through cassava, corn and coffee plantations. Men and women worked the fields. Every plantation had a few mud huts with straw roofs. It looked as if the routines were the same in every village. Men sat smoking while their women worked: digging, pounding, and grinding, babies tied to their backs. Half naked children with popped-out belly buttons and runny noses stared at the train as if it were a vision. They waved at us. We waved back.

Mum woke up to find Jaimini crawling on her. She gently pulled herself up. Rubbing her eyes, she looked around. "Where are we?" she asked, only gradually recalling that we were on the train. Once she'd had a cup of tea, she felt much better. She stood up and walked down the aisle, looking for Jagdishbhai and his family. They were nowhere to be seen.

"Maybe they are in a different carriage," she said. "We forgot to ask their carriage and seat numbers."

Everyone had a story to tell. An older couple cried about their only son. He'd left for work one morning and never returned. They'd lived in a small village near Kampala. Their son, his wife and two grandchildren all lived with them. Their son owned a business in the Chore Bazaar in Kampala.

With the rise of Amin, things had changed in their village. It was small, made up of houses built of tin and wood. When the rain came, it battered the tin roofs, making a deafening sound. You got there from the main road by taking a dirt road into the village. At night it was very dark. The few lights were on the main road. At night going out to the toilet was a scary experience.

These houses were two-in-one: business in front, living area in the back. The houses had no lights. Though the road had once been safe, that was no longer true. With Amin in power, dangers were everywhere. Each night this old couple would watch for their son's return. He had always come home safely. Then one night he didn't.

As always, he'd called before leaving his business. It usually took him a half hour to get home. They'd waited and waited. It was a foggy night, and they couldn't see any lights, not even those on the main road. Two people rode by on bicycles. Otherwise they saw no one.

They had a good relationship with their neighbors, so they went out and knocked on doors. Some neighbors went with them, using a flashlight to look along the side of the road, in case he'd had an accident or was stuck in the mud. It started raining. Between rain, fog and darkness, soon they couldn't see anything. All they could hear were the sounds of grasshoppers and frogs. After an hour they gave up. They decided their son had been wise enough to stay the night in Kampala. Talking with their neighbors, they decided if they hadn't seen him by the next day, they would go looking in Kampala.

"That night we did not sleep," the old man said. "We kept wishing it was morning. I sat the whole night dozing on a rocking stool, hearing the clock click, click, click. Every second was like years. Early the next morning, I had to knock on neighbors' doors again. At sunrise, three of us drove into Kampala.

"I prayed the whole way to the Bazaar, hoping to see my son there. But his business's windows were broken. The front door hung loosely by a single screw. The place was wide open to anyone. At this point my instinct told me that harm had come to my son. We parked and walked in. The store was emptied. There was no sign of my son. I called his name and the echo bounced back. I shivered. When I asked the neighboring business people whether they'd seen my son, they said they'd seen him come out, get in his car, then go back inside as if he'd forgotten something. There'd been rioters in the neighborhood, smashing cars and looting businesses. Perhaps he was worried about them. The neighbors expressed their best wishes for our son's safety.

"From there we drove to the home of my son's friend. This friend hadn't seen him in about ten days. My neighbor and I drove back to the Bazaar to see if we could find any sign. A young Indian boy ran towards us. He looked frightened. He gave us a signal to drive behind the building. When he showed up a few minutes later, this boy recognized me. He said he was my son's newest employee. He said, 'Yesterday evening, I was waiting for the bus when I saw your son coming out of his store with a heavy bag wrapped in his arms. I assumed it was cash. The rioters were coming closer and I heard there was no bus service. I was about to ask your son to drive me home when two black men came from behind and pushed him into his own car. I hid myself behind a car. Your son and his captors drove off. People ran past me, shouting that the rioters were beating or killing any Indians. So I ran. When I heard on the radio that the riot was over, naturally I returned here to work. I cried seeing the empty store.'

"Hearing, this news, I broke down. I couldn't bring this horrible news home to my wife and daughter-in-law. I had thoughts of suicide, but my neighbors gave me courage and hope. He could be alive somewhere, they said.

"But after few days, some locals passing through a corn field in the neighboring village came across a body. They ran to tell someone, and soon the rumor reached our village. The leader of our village commanded a group to go see if it was one of ours. They found the body, face down in some bushes. When they turned it over they recognized our son. His clothes were torn, and his body was missing a leg. He'd been trying to run away.

"They brought his body back to our village. My daughter-in-law fainted and my wife cried until her voice was gone. Since then my wife has become very quiet and ill. So I decided to leave Uganda to save the only family I have left."

With that, the old man fell silent.

CHAPTER 22

From our compartment, the sky looked like a blue dome that changed to vibrant orange and fiery yellow as the sun went down. As the sunset deepened, these hues resolved into a deep red, followed by darkness. They were the most beautiful sunset colors I'd ever seen.

When the air from the windows turned cold, Mum pulled down the shutter on her side and told us to pull down the one on our side too. She lay down, covering herself with a woolen Kashmir shawl Papa had bought for her when he'd visited India some years earlier.

"Get a blanket and cover yourselves up," Mum said, not wanting us to catch cold. Before pulling down the shutters, I took one final look at the falling darkness. I saw a few dim lights between the plantations. I assumed these were small fires burning outside the huts.

Most of the lights in our carriage had been turned off, leaving the compartments dark and silent. The only voices were the low tones of some older men talking near the front of the car. I covered Donna in a blanket and carefully laid her on the other side of my feet. I could not sleep. I sat on my knees looking back to see who else was awake.

"Don't keep looking around," Mum said, not opening her eyes. "Just turn off the light and go to sleep."

I turned off the lights and lay down, listening to the sound of the wheels rolling along the tracks. I remembered a book I'd read about two little children taking the train from London to visit their grandparents' farm. My eyes closed.

It was almost midnight when I awoke to a sudden jerk. The train thumped to a standstill. Most of the other passengers woke up. Lights came on.

Uncle Pravinbhai whispered: "We're in Tororo. This is the border. Once we get past here we're safe. We will have to show our passports."

We heard a man's voice whispering from the front row, saying he saw some trouble outside. Uncle Pravinbhai looked out the window. Soldiers surrounded the train. When we heard this we fell into total silence. The door opened. Soldiers, each holding a rifle and a stick, appeared at every compartment. We didn't move or even look at them.

Their boots clomped heavily on the floor of the car, and they spoke in Swahili, telling each other, "These Indians are very smart. We must stop them from taking gold and cash out of Uganda. If they won't listen, kill them."

One tall soldier seemed to be in charge. He walked the aisle, giving orders. Pointing his stick, he would say, "You go left and you two go on your right."

Another soldier checked passports, while his colleagues opened bags and suitcases. They snatched up any jewelry, and ordered those who were wearing rings, bracelets and necklaces to turn them over. Whenever anyone resisted, the soldiers used force. If they decided anyone looked suspicious, they pulled that passenger up from the seat, and made the passenger take off every stitch of clothing.

When one couple refused to do this, the soldiers threw them off the train. Outside more soldiers beat the couple with sticks, then kicked them, and finally shot them.

The crack of the guns terrified us. One mother held her baby's mouth to quiet her. Parents whispered to children, "Lie down and cover your ears."

As they neared our end of the car a woman ahead of us sat on her jewelry, hoping they wouldn't notice. Even with a gun pointed in her face, she denied having any valuables. The commander didn't believe her. As he squeezed both her hands another soldier grabbed the bag she was sitting on.

"Look," he said. "Pure gold sets! I will decorate my wife with these." He handed one to his commander. "Here, take this one and decorate your wife too."

"I beg you, please," said the woman. "Give me back my necklaces. They are for my brother's wedding."

They pulled her from her seat and beat her with sticks. They left her unable to stand, but she was lucky. At least they didn't throw her off the train.

Another lady hid her cash in her sari blouse. She sat with her hands folded. The soldiers wasted little time, cutting open her blouse, and finding what was there. They took everything, then slapped her until blood flowed from her mouth.

With each new assault we all wanted to shout, but none of us were brave enough, or foolish enough, to do it. Finally an older man could not take it anymore. He stood up and cried, "Take everything from all of us but leave us alone."

The soldiers looked at one another and laughed. Walking toward him, one soldier said, "How dare you talk to us like that, you little old man." They threw him off the train, stabbed him in the stomach, filled his mouth with alcohol, lit it on fire, then finally killed him.

As they beat and killed passengers, the soldiers passed suitcases full of loot out the windows.

Finally our turn was coming. As they approached, Mum breathed: "Put on your pullovers and draw your scarves around your necks."

This was a chance we had to take. Three of us were wearing a 24-carat gold necklace. These were the only negotiable assets Mum had. She would need the money they would bring for our food and school tuition in India. Mum signaled us to sit straight, keep quiet, and show no fear. Bina warned Jade softly: "Keep quiet… otherwise the bad men will kill you." Jade was an intelligent bird. He sensed the danger, and obeyed. Bina covered the cage with a bed sheet, putting bags of food on top.

Donna shivered with fear. I switched seats with her, putting her by the window, while I took the aisle seat closer to the soldiers' path. "Look down," I said. "Do that no matter what happens. I will tell you when to look up. That way, you will be safe." We all prayed for safety.

One of the men in our carriage was Balwant Singh. He was tanned, and muscular. He was a follower of Ghandi, believing in nonviolence, but all of this was too much for him. Though his seatmate cautioned him to be quiet, uncle Balwant Singh couldn't contain his anger.

Pointing his finger at them, he said, "We are finally leaving Uganda, which was a home to us. We left our houses full of furniture, cars and all our other possessions. What little we have we need for our survival. Look at these people. They are all going to a new country. How will they feed themselves and their children? What else do you want from us?"

The commander did not like people talking to him this way. He grasped Mr. Singh by his turban, and threw him on the floor. "How dare you talk to me like that?" he snapped. "Did you not see what happened to that old man? I sent him to heaven."

With that, he and the other men stabbed Mr. Singh in the head. His turban flew to one side as he tried to fight back, but it was useless. He lost consciousness. No one dared to move.

We could not do anything but sit helplessly and listen. Mum whispered to Donna and Kevin to close their eyes, pretending they were asleep. Our turn had come.

Two soldiers stood in the aisle, their backs to us. One pulled down bags, throwing the contents on the floor. The other soldier eyed uncle Pravinbhai, who had his hand in his jacket.

Uncle Pravinbhai was hiding his wedding ring. He'd tried to take it off but it was too tight. I didn't dare to move my head, but I could see them with my left eye. The soldier pulled uncle Pravinbhai's hands out from his jacket. "What are you hiding?" he demanded.

"Nothing," said uncle Pravinbhai.

The soldier saw the ring and tried to pull it off uncle Pravinbhai's finger. All that did was tear the skin. "Give me a knife," he said to his colleague. The other soldier dropped bags on the floor, reached into his pocket, and opened a sharp browning knife. He handed it to his colleague.

"Please don't hurt me," said uncle Pravinbhai. "I will give you all my money."

His wife, Neeru, had been totally silent, but now she spoke up: "Please leave my husband alone. Here, take this one." She handed over her mangalsutra pendant (a wedding symbol from uncle Pravinbhai), earrings, and bracelets.

The men laughed, and took the loot, but one kept a grip on uncle Pravinbhai's finger. In an instant the soldier severed the finger from uncle Pravinbhai's hand. Blood poured out and he screamed. His finger flew up, then dropped under Mum's bench.

When I saw that severed finger I felt nauseous. The soldiers hadn't seen its path. They were looking everywhere. One of them followed my stare, and asked, "What are you looking at?" He searched under the bench. "It is here," he told his colleague, putting the finger in his pocket. He stood up and looked at Neerumashi.

She wept as she tied a part of her sari around her husband's bleeding finger. She held it tight to stop the blood.

"You see," said one soldier. "Look at this beautiful woman. She knows her duty." He nudged uncle Pravinbhai's shoulder and laughed.

One of the soldiers turned to us. Mum held Jaimini on her lap, rocking her to sleep. She handed over our passports without looking up at the men. The soldier facing us took the passports and opened them one-by-one. As he checked the pictures he looked down at each of our faces. When he got to me he paused and stared for a moment. Fear mixed with adrenaline in my veins. I tried to hide my terror. In my mind I was determined to protect my family, though I had no idea how I could.

Finally the soldier looked at Mum. "Give me your valuables," he said.

"I do not have any," Mum replied without looking up. She kept rocking Jaimini.

"You stand up," he demanded.

I distracted him with a cough. He looked at me. He was a huge, strong man with a face dark as charcoal. He had honor badges stitched on the shoulder of his uniform. He carried a rifle and a stick. Under his cap he had short curly hair. His cunning eyes were like tiny bird's eggs with black pupils. I looked straight at him, holding my breath as my stomach tightened. I tried to mask my fear. "Mister," I said, "the only things we have are food and clothing. If you want you can have it all."

He gripped my hair and pulled me up. Hot breath spewed from his wide, hairy nostrils. I felt it on my face. I thought he was going to pull out my hair, and somehow that emboldened me.

"You little animal," he hissed, dropping me into my seat like a bag of potatoes. My neck would hurt for several days, and I would always remember those eyes. His stare shifted to Donna and Kevin.

A voice called out, "Come! It's time to go."

He spun and walked toward the train doors. The rest went with him, lugging bags crammed with valuables, as they stepped on clothing and other possessions. In Swahili they spoke of how much this stop had been worth to them.

We'd been there for less than an hour.

Finally the soldiers allowed the driver to start the engine. The door closed behind them. Everyone heaved a sigh of relief, yet now we would have to face the grief we felt for the bodies we were leaving behind. A doctor on the train treated those who'd been wounded. We repacked as well as we could.

The train moved slowly. I was tired of sitting in the same seat. "Uncle Pravin, can I come sit over there?" I asked.

"Of course," he replied.

I sat opposite Neerumashi. She'd been traumatized by the sight of her husband's severed finger, and by the loss of her wedding jewelry. Tears ran down her cheeks as she said, "Mila, you could have been in a big trouble. When that man pulled you up and looked at you, I was afraid that was the end for you. Those people were cowardly, heartless killers. You are so brave. You pushed them away."

I smiled and looked out the small window. We hadn't yet left the border. The soldiers were having their own little party, sipping Johnny Walker scotch and smoking stolen cigarettes. Clothing and suitcases were scattered across the grass between the bodies.

The train started moving again, accelerating until it reached a good cruising speed. One of the crew stood up at the front, and cried out, "We are finally out of Uganda." We all applauded.

That was followed by an announcement. The crewmember said, "Today, we all are very lucky to be alive and safe. Words seem inadequate to express the sadness we all feel about the loss of those who we had to leave behind. Please accept our heartfelt condolences to all of you who lost your loved ones. We will be reaching out to those who grieve, comforting them throughout our journey. We will remember every loss, giving respect to their souls as they travel in peace on their journey. We will perform the death rituals on the ship." When this announcement was over they turned off the lights. Some went to sleep, while others stayed up, talking in low tones in the dim light.

Before I could doze off, the train slowed down again. Fear ran through me. Were there more dangers? I looked out the window, but a thick mist obscured all but a few hazy lights. I thought I saw a platform. I did. We'd reached Malaba, the first station in Kenya.

Crowds were waiting. *What were all these people doing at a train station in the middle of the night?* I wondered. There wasn't enough room onboard for them. I'd never seen people dressed so warmly. The men wore sweaters, and women had on knitted cardigans over their saris.

As we came to a standstill, carts arrived on the platform filled with packaged food, drinks, blankets, toys, milk, and first aid items. A kerosene lamp glowed from each cart because the station's lights were dim. All the items on the carts were for us. Volunteers from Kenya's Indian community had organized this program to help refugees like us. Those of us who had little, or who lost what we'd had on the way, would now have enough to survive our escape from Amin and his men.

We could smell the dal curry and flavored rice, and our stomachs growled with hunger. The volunteers rushed from one window to the next, handing over the packages. Some listened as passengers told of our tragic experience at the border. We told how we'd had to leave our father behind.

In the surprisingly cold weather, the aroma of the food made our mouths water. We'd never seen food packaged this way, still warm, even though it hadn't yet been opened. These meals were nicely covered in aluminum wrapping paper. The puris, vegetables, rice and pickles were set out neatly between dividers. Dal, raita and jalebi were packed separately, each in a small container.

A couple of younger boys passed from seat to seat, serving tea and water. Mum filled her thermos with hot tea. Women with babies got as many baby care packages as they needed.

We thanked each and every Kenyan Indian we saw for this welcome help. The guard blew the whistle and the train engine started.

We began to open the packages.

"Watch out," Mum warned. "It's too hot."

The warm dinner was so welcome. The raita, jalebis were delicious and refreshing on the spicy food. After a good meal, the extra blankets came in handy. They were all packed in original wrapping that displayed the company's logo. A full stomach and the warm blankets made us drowsy, safe and ready for a good sleep.

I looked around. Everyone was sound asleep, except the old man's widow. She and a few others were still mourning. I covered my back with a blanket and sat on

my knees with both my hands crossed on the window frame so I could look outside. I watched as we passed Eldoret. That meant we were approaching the Equator. A strong cold breeze blew through the window, indicating that there must be water nearby. I knew from what I'd learned before that here we must be passing Lake Narasha. I would have liked to see the Timboroa forest, but it was too dark.

I was excited about the idea of being at the Equator. At exactly 2am I knew we'd reached it. It was marked on a rectangle sign mounted on a round, marble-like stone. This sat on a square flat piece of marble with a white line running from one end to another. As the train passed over this line, I wished I could touch the sign, but I had to settle for the sight of it. I wrote down my thoughts in my notebook. After that my weariness caught up with me. I fell right to sleep.

I slept well and woke up before dawn. I poked my head out and took a deep breath. The fresh breeze and the smell of the park were good enough to make me feel at peace. As we approached Nakuru, I was amazed at the unique landscape. Some of it might have been the result of soil erosion. It was like a reddish pink Grand Canyon.

I felt like I needed to go to the bathroom. Most of the passengers were still asleep. I could hear older men gargling as they brushed their teeth. It felt filthy to me. I slowly stood up, not wanting to wake the others.

As I walked towards the toilet, I saw a young man in his compartment, bent low to search for something underneath his bunk. When I heard a click, I blurted out: "What is that?"

He gave a nasty look. At the side of his foot, I saw

something that looked like the barrel of a rifle.

"Oh, my God!" I said.

He pushed it back under, and stood, giving me a threatening look. I jogged towards the toilet and pushed at the door. It wouldn't give. I kicked it. It didn't budge. I saw the young man coming towards me, his hands wide and grasping, as if he were going to get hold of me. His footfalls echoed through my head, and I heard his labored breathing. I wanted to shout, but my voice caught in my throat.

I stood still, my back towards the toilet door. He set his hands against the door, and looked down at me. "You keep your mouth shut," he said. "The rifle isn't mine. One of the soldiers dropped it—the one who pushed the couples out of the train. I saw it near my feet, so I pushed it underneath the bunk."

Once I'd listened to his story, he pushed the toilet door open for me, then went back to his seat. I closed the door behind me, and spattered cold water all over my face. I was afraid to go back out again. I was sitting down to pee when I lost my balance, and peed in my pants. As I came out with wet panties, the train jerked. I walked quickly to our compartment where my sisters were looking out the window.

"You look pale," said Donna.

I said nothing of the young man and his rifle. I kept my mouth shut as he'd told me to do.

At dawn, the train stopped at Kenya's Rift Valley Province, Nakuru station. Here volunteers had crowded the platform, even outnumbering the ones we'd seen in Malaba. Perhaps it was because this was a bigger town. The volunteers gave us the same hospitable treatment we'd received before, asking us the same questions. Again and again we repeated details of our story. Often we got emotional.

This time we got breakfast: parathas with pickles, bread with butter and cheese, chips, tea and water. We were already full from our late night dinner but we did not reject this meal. We ate most of the food, saving the rest for later. We were stopped there for forty-five minutes. By now all the passengers were awake and there was a big line near the toilet. I was glad I'd already used it.

Mum looked fresh, with her hair in a black net. The only thing she needed was a fresh rose in her hair. She sat in a lotus position reading a book. "Go brush your teeth and wash your faces," she said to my siblings. "Look at Mila. She is ready before any of you."

After three-quarters of an hour we started moving again. We passed over a bridge, then entered a vast area of small farms. As the sun rose, the sky filled with red and orange hues. It was a glorious view. We passed fields full of coffee, wheat, barley and maize. Water drops from the leaves shone like crystals in the sunlight.

On this side of the bridge the landscape was more open. Tall thin natives watched the train pass by. Prafulbhai Soni came to our part of the car to talk with uncle Pravinbhai. Uncle Soni had suffered a slight wound at the border, and was still recovering.

"Those are the Masai," he said, pointing at the natives outside the windows. "I've heard of them, but you seldom see them in their traditional clothing."

The clothing he spoke of was ochre. They wore beaded jewelry around their necks, arms and legs. Each of them also wore a garment knotted around one shoulder, which came down, covering the body. The men held spears. Their skin looked soft, and their backs were straight. They were said to have great stamina and courage. I didn't see any huts nearby. *What are they doing in the middle of nowhere?* I wondered. *How far do they have to walk to their huts?* As if in reply to my thought, a few cattle dung huts came into view.

That morning the girls from the next compartment came to play cards. We made space for them to sit. We were playing the game where the winners get to sing their favorite song. The older ladies heard us singing and joined us, and we switched from card games to playing the singing game, Antakshari. The boys got into it, reaching out to drum on the metal sides of the train. We made more friends, bonding with each other. It was fun. The time passed faster than we knew. Looking outside, we saw giraffes, huge mountains, landscapes that revealed a volcanic past, and Mount Longonot rising from the Rift Valley floor.

CHAPTER 23

A little past noon, the train stopped at Naivasha station. Our new friends went back to their seats as we were all given lunch packages. The food was delicious, with fresh pickles. At each station Mum filled the thermos with warm tea. The tea was like an addiction for Mum. She would get headaches if she didn't have strong masala tea at least twice a day. I couldn't get it past my throat. After lunch Mum went to see the other women she'd befriended. Bina cleaned Jade's cage and refreshed his food and water.

Some children saw Jade, and asked if they could play with him.

"You stand there and just watch while I clean the cage," Bina told them, but they wouldn't listen. They tried to feed Jade biscuits. Some stuck their fingers into the cage.

"The parrot will bite you," said Bina.

The children moved back, watching from a distance. Still they asked many questions.

"What does he eat?" one child asked.

"Does he sleep at night?" another inquired.

"Look," said Bina, taking a handful of grain. "He eats this."

"He eats this," Jade repeated over and over.

"She is talking," said a little boy, laughing as he mimicked the bird.

With lunch over, the girls came back to play. My sisters were more interested in playing than listening to me; I sat by the window watching the scenery. The unusual green landscape gave way to the Great Rift Valley. Here tectonic shifts had cleaved the plains, along with the ancient volcanoes that had shaped this land. I watched the hazy blue valley and the velvet mountains of Longonot Park pass by as we neared Limuru. I was fortunate enough to see some giraffes close to the trees. With their long necks, they could reach the leaves on those tall trees. It seemed like party time for the giraffe family.

I felt sleepy but I wanted to see it all. What if we were to pass a herd of zebras chasing an antelope? I laid my head on the window frame, counting the electricity pylons. My eyes closed. I was awakened by the sound of a neighbor's baby crying. We were passing through many small stations and villages. There were a lot more huts than brick houses.

As the train wound around the big curve before the Limuru Tunnel, I stuck my head out to see the whole train from front to back. Children were hanging out every train window, waving, screaming and calling to each other. The wind blew our words away into the valley. At the sight of so many children, my heart leapt.

As we neared Nairobi, most of the Kenyan natives were dressed differently than those in Uganda. Women were colorfully dressed in the African Islamic style, covering their heads with sjaals. Men wore round hats, top shirts and matching loose pants.

The train slowed down as it passed Kikuyu station. That's when we first saw Mount Kenya, the second highest mountain in Africa. The late evening sun shone on the snow covering the ragged peaks. It was like white icing on a cake. Below the snow green slopes ran down, thick with small bushes. Further down the landscape appeared to be dryer. Stubby acacia trees dotted the landscape, looking like flat umbrellas. I'd seen pictures of Mount Kenya in books, but here it was, right in front of me. Wow!

The train slowed as it passed mud huts and cornfields on the outskirts of Nairobi. *If Nairobi is such a modern city, how could it have all these mud huts?* I wondered.

We reached Nairobi, Kenya's capital, late that afternoon. We were in southern Kenya now, over a mile above sea level. From our compartment, the city below looked clean and modest. The platform at the train station was much wider than those we'd seen, and more Indian volunteers were there to meet us. These people looked more sophisticated, as happens in the biggest cities. Indian ladies wore colorful knitted cardigans over elegant saris. Their gifts included extra sweet desserts, nuts, snacks and sodas, as well as dinner. Some passengers had family in Kenya. These people passed from one coach to the next, asking if we knew their kin. I could barely hear the names for all the noise.

Uncle Soni jumped up from his seat. "Yesterday morning, before I left, I called my sister," he said. "There she is. Look, my niece and nephews. Mala! Mala!" he called. He could not wait. He tried to open the door, but it seemed stuck.

"We are not allowed to get out of the train until we reach Mombasa," said another man.

As uncle Soni prepared to jump out the window, we tried to stop him. "The train will pull off without you."

"We have twenty minutes," he said. "I'll be back."

When we were five minutes from departure we all got worried. Mum told us to watch for him. "If he misses this train, leaving Kenya will become much more difficult for him. All his papers are here."

"There he is," shouted a girl in the next compartment, but it was the wrong man.

"That's not him," I said.

"The ticket guard blew the whistle. Didn't Mr. Soni hear it?

"There, he is!" cried Kevin.

Uncle Soni was still with his sister and nieces. They were saying an emotional goodbye.

"Uncle Soni! Uncle Soni!" we shouted. "Hurry up! The train is going to leave." He didn't hear us.

We asked one of the tea servers to get him. The boy put down his tea can and ran to uncle Soni. The third whistle blew. The train started. The boy grasped uncle Soni's hands, and dragged him towards the moving train. Uncle Soni's sister cried. Uncle Soni got hold of the window and tried to pull himself in. We shouted: "Uncle Pravin! Help us!" forgetting he had a severe fever. Several men came to our rescue, grasping uncle Soni's arms. They pulled, while the tea-serving boy outside pushed. Finally there was uncle Soni, inside the train.

"Oh, I made it," he said, smashing his nose on the bunk.

Mum was angry. "How can you ever do something like this? You could have talked to your sister from the compartment. What would have happened if the train left without you?"

"I'm sorry," he said. "You see, my sister and I were very close, growing up without our mother. Please understand.

My leaving for India is hard for both of us. Living in Uganda I could see her twice a year, but India is far away, and we are not wealthy. She can't afford the ticket to come visit me there." Tears welled up in his eyes. "I don't know if I will ever see my sister and my nieces again."

An older wise man standing next to uncle Soni said: "Soniji, feel blessed. At least you are alive. You were able to see your sister today, and you will again, someday soon. Remember what happened to the ones the soldiers killed at the border. We are all lucky."

Mr. Soni wiped away his tears. "Yes," he said, "you are absolutely right. Do you have an aspirin? I have a headache."

"Here," Mum said, "take this aspirin, and here is a glass of water."

Mr. Soni fell silent, and remained that way the whole evening. Up until then he'd been in good humor, telling jokes, and providing fun for all of us. Now he was sad.

Though I wasn't hungry, once I smelled the delicious dinner, I couldn't resist eating. I ate a little of everything and kept the rest for later. Sitting in a lotus position, Mum enjoyed her meal, feeding small mouthfuls to Jaimini.

When Kevin came near me, I pulled him onto my lap and held him tight.

"Look," he said, pointing outside. "A lion." He was right. A lion was resting under a tree.

"There should be a lioness nearby," I said. I called my sisters to come and have a look, but they were too busy playing cards with their friends.

"Where is the lioness?" Kevin asked.

I caught sight of her, and pointed. "There."

"Oh, yes."

We both gazed at the animals as we passed them. I pulled Kevin higher in the seat. We could see the lioness standing there staring at a herd of antelope. I was amazed that she didn't attack them. Kevin and I kept watch for hours, noting any wildlife that was new to us. Ostriches proudly strutted, displaying their beautiful pink and blue feathers.

Eventually it was time for Antakshari. We could hear the songs vibrating from the other compartments.

Late in the evening, when they dimmed the lights, an elderly lady complained: "Hey, you girls, let me and the others get some sleep." We quieted down. Mum told us to put on our sweaters. It was getting cold. Chandrika invited us to join her and her friends playing cards. Carrying my blanket, I visited with them, even though I felt sleepy.

Chandrika was fun. She dressed well, wearing a silk sari. She pinned her sari drape to her blouse with a colorful broach. Her thick shining hair hung in curls around her ears. She often led us through different games and Qawwali songs, her eyes twinkling.

It was almost midnight and my eyes started closing. "I should go to sleep," I said.

"Play one more game," Chandrika insisted.

The girls also wanted me to stay. "It is fun with you," they said.

I stayed until everyone felt sleepy. By then I was exhausted. All the late nights were catching up with me. Yet, when I closed my eyes, everything came back to me: Uncle Soni almost missing the train, Uncle Pravinbhai's chopped-off finger under the bunk, and that army officer looking straight into my eyes. My whole body felt like a stone. Donna's foot moved, settling near my face. It smelled awful.

I found myself wondering why we had to endure these things. I missed my cozy bed. I wanted so much to sleep in my own bed. I stifled a sob.

"What is it?" Mum asked.

"Nothing."

"Then why are you not asleep? It's late."

I wiped my nose with the bed sheet, and went to sleep. Soon enough I was snoring.

I woke up in the middle of the night. Something was shaking us. Was it an earthquake? The train was jerking to a stop. Others were waking up too. In those first moments of consciousness most of us were scared. Many still feared a repetition of our experience at the border. Though we were now in a safer country, our fear seemed reflexive whenever the train stopped unexpectedly at night.

"What is it?" asked Lalitamashi Chandarana.

I lay listening. Some lights were still on. Mum covered her face with her sari and went back to sleep. From the smell of the forest and the sound of the river flowing, I knew we were probably in a national park. I knew we were passing through the lands of the Masai tribes. In school I'd heard that Masians like to drink fresh animal blood, and that they killed many workers when this railway was being built.

A guard came through the car, looking for volunteers to help with a task. "You need not worry," he said. "There's a dead animal on the railroad."

"Oh, thank God," whispered Lalita. She wiped sweat from her face with her dress, then fell back to sleep.

Chandrikamashi looked at her. "I'm glad she went back to sleep," she said. "She always creates drama." She was right. Lalita was an unfriendly, sarcastic and demanding girl.

Though some of us peered out our windows, it was too dark to see. Many of us felt haunted. We wondered: who would want to go outside at this time of the night? An animal might eat you. The trees were utterly still in the calm night air. We could hear the movements of animals. Some must have been predators, and some would be stalking their prey. If we looked hard enough into the darkness, our imaginations made it seem as if eyes were glimmering from every tree. Someone on the train told the story of a lion that had killed many of the workers who'd built this railway back in 1898. Were their ghosts haunting us?

"We need to help," said Mr. Singh. "Otherwise we will be stuck here all night." Once some big torches provided light, a few brave men jumped out. Now the boy brought out his hidden rifle, and handed it over to the guard.

"Where did you get this?" the guard asked him.

The boy explained to the guard's satisfaction.

The rifle came in handy. The dead animal blocking the tracks was a baby water buffalo. While the men managed to clear it off the track, they made noise, got hot, and sweated. The smells and sounds attracted more animals. The guards were ready to shoot if necessary.

Finally, a half hour later, we started again. We hoped to reach Mombasa by four in the afternoon.

This time all the lights went out, and we all fell to sleep. As dreams overwhelmed me, I realized I was lost in a jungle. A lion stalked me and started to roar. I stood still. When he roared again, I ran. He chased me and I climbed a tree. I had no way of getting down. As this lion kept staring at me, I felt myself sweating. "Go away!" I snapped. "Go away."

Suddenly I woke up. Kevin had tossed water in my face. "Go away," I ordered him. "Let me sleep." I covered my face. Kevin pulled the cover away. I pulled him up, and covered him in my blanket. He liked it.

As we lay there, Kevin told stories about what he would do in India. He would go to a good school, get a college degree, and earn lots of money. As he prattled on, we both fell asleep. When I woke we were reaching Makindu Station. People were getting ready. Soon there would be breakfast packages.

CHAPTER 24

I'd had enough of this journey. I didn't care to brush my teeth for lunch. At these later stops the volunteers wore clothes that were much different than what we'd seen in Nairobi. The ladies wore simple saris, while the men had on light colored pants. Most of them also wore thin shirts. I assumed this was due to the warm weather. Among them were some Sikh volunteers.

After lunch, I brushed my teeth, washed my face and put on my new dress.

Mum said, "Tie all the blankets in this bed sheet, put them underneath the seats, and make space for the suitcases."

We took down our suitcases from the overhead compartment. As Donna folded the blankets, I put them underneath the bunks.

A shrewd but smelly woman named Ansurya Ganjawala stopped to ask, "What are you hiding?" Her lips pursed, and she burped.

"Just making space," I said. She smelled like onions and garlic.

"Oh, I see," she said, and left. Our whole place smelled after she left. No one liked talking to Ansuryamashi.

"Mum," I said, "my knees are dirty."

"Here," she said, giving me a piece of wet cloth to wipe the dirt away.

We were nearing the end of the train ride. It was Friday the 3rd of November.

When I found uncle Pravin, he moved to the aisle seat, giving me his by the window.

His wife, Neelumashi, was sad. "Today is Dhanteras," she said.

"What's that?" I asked.

"It's the first day of the Diwali festival," she said. "We worship the goddess of wealth so she will bring us prosperity and well-being. I wish I had my jewelry; I would have worshipped them with water rituals."

One of our neighbors handed over some shillings. "Worship these," he said. "They will bring prosperity."

Neelumashi and our neighbors chatted about the Diwali festival, as I watched the scenery go by. I had quite a view. We were rolling through what looked like a desert. Small trees and thorny brush covered this side of the plain. Gray-green creepers, red dirt roads, and rocky, wooded hills dominated a view that was entirely unfamiliar to me. Elephants, giraffes, rhinoceroses, lions, leopards, and impalas lived here.

We were entering Tsavo National Park. I took Kevin in my lap. "Look," I said, pointing out an elephant followed by its baby.

"Look," Kevin said, pointing. "More elephants." A herd of tusked, reddish-brown elephants approached. I had never seen elephants that color. They emerged from one place in the bushes, then disappeared into another. Once they were gone, Kevin left.

Not long after that a huge mountain came into view. Two peaks were covered with snow. Clouds shrouded parts of the mountain. *Which one could it be?* I wondered. Then I got it. This was Mount Kilimanjaro, the highest mountain in Africa. It was sometimes called "the roof of Africa." I was unable to see the whole of it, but I was lucky to catch this glimpse. I took out my notebook and wrote it down.

When I switched to the other side of the car, I saw an impala jump out from the bushes, then run at full speed.

Finally we slowed down. I assumed we were nearing Mombasa. We were in a dry land where they grew cashew trees. I wanted to see how Mombasa looked, but uncle Pravin corrected me. "Mila," he said, "we still have a few more hours to go. Be patient."

"Then why is the train slowing down?" I asked.

"I have no idea," he admitted.

As we approached the ocean the air grew humid, but I wondered why we were sweating. Wasn't the ocean supposed to bring fresh winds?

It was 11am. I wished we could stop and pick cashews. Suddenly I saw something like a dark ball bounce outside the train. Someone pulled the emergency chain, and the train suddenly stopped. "What's going on?" everyone asked.

A three-year-old boy from a neighboring compartment had fallen out of the train. His sisters were screaming: "Help! Help!" His mother cried: "Look! There's my baby! Someone please help me!"

She started beating her elder daughter for being careless. "How did this happen?" screamed the mother.

The girl was sobbing. "I had him in my arms, but he climbed up my chest. Somehow he slipped from my grasp."

"My baby! My baby!" cried his mother. "Please, someone help me." After some men made an unsuccessful attempt to force the door open, the driver unlocked it, and the men jumped down. The baby's mother threw a blanket outside. They put the crying baby in the blanket, and brought him back to his mum.

A doctor on board checked the baby. "Poor little boy," he said holding the baby on his lap. The baby's forehead was bleeding. The doctor cleaned the cut, bandaged the baby's head, then cleaned the other cuts and bruises. When he was done, he told the baby's mum, "Let him rest for now. Do not shake nor move him. I'll give you some medicine, but if any complications come up, take him to the hospital in Mombasa." He turned to the baby's sisters. "You're all lucky this train was moving so slowly. That's the only reason your brother survived."

As he left, the mum was giving the baby a bottle of warm milk.

People were getting impatient. They spent their time pulling out luggage, repacking, and gossiping with other passengers. Some people paced through the cars, looking out the windows. They'd had enough of this train. They were ready to move on.

After we'd had lunch, Mum gathered all our belongings, repacking everything. I looked out the window at my last views of East Africa. No fresh air blew over us here. The air was humid, and we were getting more and more sweaty and thirsty. All the water bottles were empty. I grumbled as I hallucinated. I thought I could drink all the water from the ocean. I had no idea that ocean water isn't drinkable. The train slowed. I kept an anxious watch for the town. *Will Mombasa be like Kampala?* I wondered. I didn't see any houses, yet suddenly there we were at the final stop: Mombasa harbor.

Everyone applauded. "We made it! We made it!" people cried. Still we had to wait another half hour before they opened the doors. One-by-one passengers stepped out on the platform, carrying all their luggage. Mum made sure we all carried whatever we could. As we alit on solid ground for the first time in over two days, we felt as if we'd been freed from a cage.

"Wow! Look at that!" I said. There at the dock, floating in the glittering waters of the Indian Ocean, stood the ship, *Haryana*, five-stories high. She was one of India's biggest cruise ships, and she was waiting to carry us across the ocean to the Indian subcontinent. I stood staring, unable to take my eyes off her. As I wondered what it was like onboard, I once again wished Papa was with us.

"Don't stare," said Mum. "Follow me. We need to get in a queue. Look, the line is already getting longer." Carrying a bag, her purse, and Jaimini, Mum walked with labored steps, as if she were on a treadmill. As she got into the queue, we followed. With the length of the line ahead of us, we thought it would take the whole evening. Luckily we moved ahead quickly. All they were doing was checking the passports.

The check-in counters were outside. Most of the officers were Indians. Mum pulled our passports from her purse so they could stamp them, then she checked in our extra blankets.

We found food and refreshment tables already set for us.

"Come, let's get water first," Bina called.

"Bring a glass for me too," said Mum.

I drank three glasses of water, one after another. The food looked delicious: North Indian cuisine. Despite the heat, I ate half a piece of roti and vegetables. The tea table held bowls of cashews in different flavors: salty, spicy, regular and roasted. My eyes widened and my mouth watered. They looked yummy. I ate as much as I could and filled my pockets for later. Then we sat waiting for the first and second class passengers to board.

From where we stood, we could see the whole ship. A huge anchor held it in position. There was a lot going on. The luggage went into a crate, which loaded it into the area below the decks. White-uniformed officers and crew walked from one place to another, checking every detail. There were maintenance men, engineers, and sailors. All were ensuring the ship was ready and safe for our voyage to India. On the top deck, in a small glass cabin, officers checked the ship's navigation instruments.

Bina pointed at an officer up in the glass cabin. "I think that's the captain."

"Ow!" cried Donna. "He looks like Captain Hook."

"No, he does not," I said. This man was fair, tall, and muscular, and had a salt-and-pepper beard. He looked as if he might be from northern India.

I wanted to go stand with the first and second class passengers. "We have to wait," Mum said, but I wouldn't listen. Though we were in the last of the three classes, I wanted to be the first one to board. I approached the boarding personnel.

"You have to wait," said the officer in charge.

"Oh, sorry," I said. I walked away, holding my head high.

Kevin laughed. Mum pursed her lips, and said: "You never listen."

They blew the first horn at six-thirty that evening. It was a wonderful blast, blowing smoke from the funnel-shaped horn. They connected the gangplank. First and second class passengers boarded. The crew turned on the lights, and the whole ship glowed. We picked up our carry-on bags, waiting our turn.

Passengers crowded the gangplank, forming two rows. Everyone wanted to board as fast as possible. Sailors stood at every corner, ready to direct us. They pointed to our deck and our area. We were in a huge space above the luggage hold under the hull. The beds were arranged in rows of lower and upper berths, each with a mattress and pillow. We had to bring our own bedding. The toilet and bathroom were for all of us, and the ventilation was poor. This was third class. Papa had reserved two sets of berths for six of us. Our bunks were close to the stairs going up to the deck. First and second class were above the deck, with private cabins, each with a small balcony overlooking the ocean.

We dropped our luggage on our beds.

"Come, Bina, Donna, Kevin," I said. "Let's go." While Mum got our things put away, we ran up to the deck.

Mum had brought soap, and now she refreshed herself, changing her sari, then settling back with a book. She had no interest in seeing the ocean. She would be satisfied to hear us describe it. She'd sailed this route before when Bina and I were babies. That had been in a much smaller ship, and Mum had told me how I'd been seasick through the whole voyage. They'd thought I was going to die. Now I wondered if her apathy toward the sights was rooted in missing Papa.

We were excited. We wanted to see what the world looked like from a ship. We were going to be here for nine days, and we wanted to get our bearings.

The deck was crowded, and I soon realized that most of these passengers weren't Kenyans. They were Ugandan refugees like us, fleeing Amin. I had no idea there had been so many of us on the train. We squeezed in to get to the railing. Down below on the dock people stood, waiting to see the ship off.

They pulled the anchor, removed the gangplank, and the second horn blew. A while after that the third horn sounded, along with more smoke. By seven pm the *Haryana* was ready, and we sailed slowly out of the harbor. The people onshore waved, and we waved back.

I followed my sisters and my brother, and we called out: "Good-bye East Africa!" Other children joined our call. As I saw the shore fading away, I felt a chill run down my spine. At my core I felt a profound sadness. Africa was all of my memories. It was my childhood, my home, and my youthful paradise. All of my identity had been formed here. I recalled when I was little more than a baby, and we lived on the Uganda-Congo border. I'd been only 2. We walked home late after visiting friends. Papa carried me on his shoulders while Bina walked beside us. There was no fear. No one tried to harm us.

The Africans had been innocent. We children had played outside in the garden all the time. We drove a toy car on the bridge over the river, and walked through the forest to pick carrots from our friends' farm. I learned to understand the value of people, culture, and country. I'd thought of Uganda, "the pearl of East Africa," as home.

As the people on the dock shrank to tiny specks, lights dotted the falling darkness, defining the town of Mombasa and the East African coast. The coastline conformed with maps we'd seen. On that warm night we stood on the deck, watching as the coastline disappeared in the sunset. Soon we were surrounded only by water. In the darkness the ocean looked frightening, but soon the moonlight brought visibility. I sat holding the rails as I watched the reflection of the moon jumping in and out of the big waves.

By eleven that night, there were only a few passengers on deck. I started yawning, and headed for the stairs to our quarters. When I saw some people heading for the galley, I followed. I found people having tea and snacks. This was a welcome treat.

The galley wasn't far from our berths. It was a large space with metal dining tables and benches. They were attached to the floor to keep them from sliding in rough seas. The stoves were on the floor.

There I found uncle Soni. "Mila," he called, "come." I sat next to him. "Here, have these," he said. "They're delicious with tea. My sister made them especially for me." He began telling stories about his sister.

I didn't listen. I was watching how the cooks held the big pot with both their hands, pouring the tea through a strainer. I had to laugh at one cook's outfit. He wore a dhoti with a light cotton top, Jape Mala (prayer beads) on his neck, and an orange kitchen towel draped over one of his shoulders. He was whistling and singing old Hindi songs. He seemed wide awake despite the hour. His dark eyebrows and mustache reminded me of the old Indian movie comedian, Mehmood. He looked just like him, so much so that he might've been Mehmood's twin. I started laughing, and tea spewed from my mouth.

The cook approached me, having no idea why I was laughing so hard. He and the others started laughing too.

"What is so funny?" he asked.

Speaking broken Hindi, I told him, "You look like Mehmood."

Speaking to everyone, including me, he said, "I am Tulsidas." He took a seat next to us and told jokes for well over an hour. It was getting late.

"I have to go," I said. "I want to explore the rest of the ship tomorrow."

"Wait," he said. "Listen to one more." I sat down my eyes half open, but I barely heard his last joke. Maybe the joke was on me. I was half asleep. He cleaned the table after everyone left. Finally the lights went off.

I was very tired and slept right away.

CHAPTER 25

When I woke up the other berths were empty. *Where are they?* I wondered. It was almost ten in the morning. I ran to the bathroom. Did I have to wash myself here? The so-called bathroom hadn't been cleaned. Water was spattered all over the floor. Luckily there was a hook for my clothes, but the water wasn't hot at all.

I got myself together, and ran to the kitchen for breakfast.

"Hello Tulsidas," I said.

"You are late," he told me.

I knew I would be grumpy all day without breakfast. I'd been told that the ship had many rules and regulations, including ones covering mealtimes, but I hadn't paid much attention.

Tulsidas saw I was upset. He put his hand on my shoulder. "Sit here my daughter. I will make fresh tea for you." He gave me leftover puris with tea. I thanked him and went on deck to find the others.

It was hot but there was an ocean breeze, so many people stayed on deck. Some sat on stools talking, while others played cards, and other stood at the railings, watching the sea. The deck seemed as big as a football field. After awhile my legs hurt from walking all over the place.

Mum was with a group of ladies. That day was Kali Chaudas, so Mum rubbed Kajal in both my eyes, making them black. She did this with all of us to abolish the laziness and evil that create so much misery in our lives. Mum said she could not concentrate. She was thinking of Papa every moment. What was he doing? Was he okay? She missed him badly.

Some people were praying for the safety of those who had stayed behind in Uganda. They chanted sacred songs and performed a water ritual, with an offering to the Indian Ocean, paying last respects to those who'd been killed and left behind.

I went looking for my sisters. They were in the shade under the lifeboat with some new friends. I sat with them and told them about Tulsidas.

"You need to watch out, Mila," said one of the older girls. "You're innocent."

"But, why?" I asked. "What's wrong with him?" I couldn't understand.

I went to the bow of the ship, climbed a rail, and put my head out to see the big waves. They broke around the ship's hull as we moved ahead. I stood there until my stomach growled, then I went mid-deck, looked up at five stories of cabins, and wondered: *Who are fortunate enough to stay up there?* They had their own veranda and a steward.

The captain stood with some of the sailors, looking down towards the deck. I waved at them. They waved back at me. At once, I felt important. I decided I would ask him to let me see the whole ship top-to-bottom. As the sun grew hot, I ran to the galley to get a glass of water.

"Oh, my God," I said to myself. "This place is baking." There was little ventilation. How could they stand it?

That's when I realized why all the cooks carried cloths on their shoulders—to wipe the sweat away.

With the help of a co-worker, Tulsidas put vegetables into a big huge pot. Two other helpers sat next to a burner that held a big frying pan filled with oil. One of these helpers rolled the puris while the other filled them. Next to them was a huge pile of dough ready to be rolled and fried. They were fast, but I wondered how long it would take them to roll it all.

I sympathized with them. These four cooks had to prepare food for over 1300 passengers. I asked one cook if my friends and I could help them. They told me to get permission from Tulsidas, who was the head cook.

Tulsidas was glad to have the extra hands. "Gophaldas, Maganlal," he ordered his helpers, "make space for the girls. They will help you roll the puris."

"I'll be right back," I said. I ran onto the deck. "Come," I called to Bina and her friends. "Let's help in the kitchen."

Three of them agreed, but Lalita didn't. She was the lazy one—always tired. We ran down the stairs. They gave each of us a rolling pin. We rolled the small round shapes of wheat dough, using flour, so they would not stick. This wasn't at all like doing it at home. The huge frying pan held at least 50 puris at a time. By the time one batch was coming out, another round had to go in. There was no waste of time or heat. Four of us rolled while a cook kept frying.

From that day on, we helped the cooks every noon and in the evenings. Other girls and ladies watched, and wanted to try it. There was so much interest that we had to take turns.

Out in the middle of the Indian Ocean the days were hot. We were always looking for shady spots. I carried a book and did some reading. I don't remember the title.

We spent most of our time on deck, making friends, and playing games. We played the singing game, Antkashari, as well as hide-and-seek, cards, or garbas (dancing).

That evening, after dinner Bhanumashi arranged a garba evening. She knew the dances, and was a good singer too. Anyone interested could join.

Garbas are traditional Gujarati folk dances. Most women and girls in India love this. Quite a few attended the first evening. The sky was bright and the moon was nearly full. It looked beautiful.

Bhanumashi told us the rules: "The dance will start every evening at exactly nine pm, and will end at eleven pm. Women, you can come in your own cultural dress. Girls, you can come with your regular dress."

On that first evening there were no men. They were talking and playing cards. They thought of garbas as something that was only done in the temple. Bhanumashi said: "That's fine. We ladies will have more fun without them." She led the first song.

All the songs were energetic. They might've been even livelier if we'd had the right musical instruments. Some women from northern India had a difficult time with the dances, and had to drop out. This was a Gujarati dance. What we did on that first night became the tradition for the rest of our sea voyage. Bina, our friends, and I attended the first few nights, but then we got bored. The songs were always the same, and there were other things we could do.

Wanting to explore, I walked everywhere. When a place was off-limits, I waited until no one was looking and sneaked in. I ducked under the rope separating us from the private areas. I went down a corridor in the sailors' quarters, and found a bunch of kids smoking cigarettes. When they saw me coming they tried to hide, putting their lit cigarettes out of sight.

One boy was careless about this, and set his pants on fire. He ran down the corridor screaming in pain, which brought a sailor out from his cabin.

"What are you all doing here?" the sailor demanded. "This is a private area. You're not supposed to be here." He rolled the boy into a blanket on the floor, suppressing the flames, then he got the boy's pants off. Another sailor brought water. The boy's upper legs had slight burns, but nothing that couldn't be treated with a standard first aid box. They put cream on the burns. The boy asked his friends to get him his shorts, hoping he could keep his parents from finding out. All of the boys were reported to the captain, who let them off with a warning.

We spent Diwali Day on board. This is a festival of lights celebrating the triumph of good over evil. We had a special lunch, followed by gheer (rice pudding) for desert. An old man wobbled by, saying it was too bad we didn't have fireworks.

That night they set up a projector on the dining table in the kitchen, and showed a Hindi movie. We sat on a covering on the floor and watched. I brought a pillow.

Once they had everything working, the film finally started. It had been made in 1969, and was called "Do Raaste", which means "two roads." It starred Rajesh Khanna and Mumtaz. Rajesh Khanna was a dutiful son and Mumtaz was his love. It was about the trials and tribulations of a lower-middle-class family. It emphasized respect for elders, the paramount status of a mother, the sanctity of family, and relationships that are sometimes stronger than blood ties.

During the intermission we got tea and snacks. One of the assistant cooks called this tea a "very special one". It was strong with crushed ginger and garam masala. Yummy, yes, but too spicy for me. The movie ended with the young lovers getting married and living happily ever after. This young couple said they learned a lesson from their parents, who had reunited.

By the fourth day Tulsidas was accustomed to me arriving late for breakfast. He kept tea and puris for me. That morning I asked him if there would be another movie that night.

"No," he said. "That happens only on Saturday and Wednesday."

I thought I might spend that night with the women dancing the garbas, but by the end of the day my feet hurt too much, so I went straight to bed.

The night was hot. I covered myself half with a bed sheet and fell to sleep right away. I dreamed that huge waves started rising up around us. The ship was sinking. Everyone put on life jackets, but when we tried to go onto the deck, the narrow stairs got crowded. Everyone was pushing each other. The passengers panicked. The ship's horns blew. Up on the deck, the first and second class passengers were running this way and that, like chickens with their heads cut off. The crew lowered lifeboats. I grew frightened. My bed shifted with the waves. I couldn't breathe. My hand went up to my throat. There I felt someone else's hand.

I suddenly woke up to find a man trying to steal my golden necklace right off my neck. I screamed as loud as I could, waking everyone. The thief ran towards the stairs. Finally a cook caught him. The thief fell down the stairs. They subdued him, and put him under a secure watch for the rest of the voyage. When they searched his quarters they found many items that had vanished earlier. These were returned to their owners.

As days passed, we made more and more friends. We shared stories of our lives, our schools and our futures. We also exchanged addresses of where we would live— places we'd never seen.

I was a young, naïve girl, with little understanding of romance. Though I thought the sailors and officers looked cute and disciplined in their caps and white uniforms, I was also shy. I couldn't flirt with the young sailors the way some other girls did.

Rumors spread about the sailors and some girls. There seemed to be a competition between the upper deck girls and those from the lower deck. It was easier for the girls in first and second class, because the sailors were usually up there. I hardly saw them on our deck.

It all got quite emotional. One girl I knew, Smita, got depressed when she discovered that her sailor friend was flirting with one of her best friends, Hansa. Hansa had an attitude. Though she was a year younger than Smita, she was a selfish know-it-all.

More than anything I wanted to see those upper decks and the first and second class accommodations. I wanted to know what they had up there. Part of this was my youthful urge to learn everything I could about the ship. What were their cabins like? Were their berths much nicer? Also, I wanted to stand way up there, on the ship's highest perch, and have a view of the entire ship and ocean. If I could get there, I wanted to shout as loud as I could, to see where the sound might go.

I wanted to talk to the captain about this, but I was too shy and scared. Whenever, I saw him on the deck, I pulled back. Finally one morning just as he came down, I drew up all my courage and approached him. He gave me a stern look. I was too afraid to make a direct request. Instead I tried starting out with some conversation about another subject.

"Are we in the middle of the ocean, sir?" I asked him.

"Yes," he replied. "Are you enjoying your journey?"

"Yes," I said, and I knew this was my chance. "Sir, there is one thing I wanted to see."

"What do you want to see?" he asked.

I plunged on toward my question, "I see you and the sailors on the top floor all the time. It would be a gorgeous to see the ocean from there."

He shook his head. "There's nothing to see other than the same water you see from here."

"I'd just like to see what it feels like to stand up there on top," I said.

"I'm sorry," said the Captain. "We have to live by a lot of rules and regulations, and that means I can't let you all go up there. There's nothing I can do to change it." With that he left.

I was upset with the Captain and his rules. I said to myself: "I'm going to get up there somehow, whether I'm allowed to or not."

That afternoon after lunch, when most of the passengers were having their afternoon naps, I sneaked up to the upper decks. It was an hour when I knew the Captain and crew were otherwise occupied. As I climbed up there, I saw a sign at the stairs, saying: "Private." I decided I hadn't really seen it, so I had no reason to stop.

When I got there I tried to walk the way a first class passenger would walk. In fact I was scared. What if someone saw me, and knew I shouldn't be there? They would throw me out.

With my head held high, I walked past the cabin doors, taking in what I could with my peripheral vision. Some passengers were napping, while others were reading. A few cabins appeared to be empty. I stopped and looked inside one of these. I'd never stayed in a 5-star hotel, but I knew this was what it must be like: a nice bed, table, and chair, along with a clothes cabinet, pretty curtains, and its own bathroom. "Wow!" I said to myself, then I climbed to the highest decks.

The ocean view from the top deck was magnificent. As I stood there staring, I didn't want to move. I lost myself in gazing at the ocean, and decided to stay to watch the sunset. The ocean was huge and there was no end to it. The sun passed through a huge sky, and would soon set over the water. I wished Papa had been able to afford to buy us tickets for a cabin up here. The vast seascape was empty. There were neither ships nor birds.

I wanted to shout to see how far my voice would go. I closed my eyes and inhaled fresh ocean air.

Suddenly I heard the captain's voice: "Hey, girl! Get out of there! Right now!"

A sailor came out from the office. "What is it, sir?" he asked.

The captain pointed at me. "She's from the deck class. She has to leave right now." Having said that, he retired to his cabin.

Unaware of the sailor following me, I started down towards our deck. Then I heard him shout: "You! Why are you still up here? You need to leave now!" He ran after me.

As I tried to escape I lost my way. When I spotted an older passenger coming out onto the veranda, I asked him: "Where are the stairs?"

"There," he said, pointing. I ran down, taking two stairs at a time, holding the bars tight so I wouldn't fall. I knocked down the "Private" sign, causing the sailor to trip over it. I ran straight to my bed and covered myself with a blanket.

"What's all this about?" Mum asked. I peered out from beneath my blanket.

The sailor kept looking for me. He asked Tulsidas if he'd seen a girl running. Though Tulsidas had seen me, he kept a straight face, and said, "No."

That night during dinner I told Tulsidas what had happened. He laughed. "It's too bad the Captain couldn't let you stay a little longer," said Tulsidas, "but he has to perform his duties."

CHAPTER 26

On the sixth day of the voyage I stayed in bed reading a book.

"Are you feeling okay?" Mum asked.

"Oh, yes," I replied.

"Then why are you still in bed?"

"I need to finish reading this book," I said. I didn't want to tell her the truth: that I was afraid the Captain would see me. I was sure if he or any of the sailors caught me, I would be punished.

Meanwhile we were sailing into a storm. Donna had been seasick ever since we'd left the harbor. Now she lay in bed the whole day, not wanting to eat anything. When she did eat something she threw up. She wasn't alone. Our whole section of berths had a foul odor from people throwing up.

We also had a bird to look after. It was time for Jade's wings to be trimmed. As Bina prepared to take the cage up on the deck, she said: "Help me carry his food and cleaning supplies."

I still didn't want to go out in the open. "I have to finish reading this book," I told her.

"What's going on with you?" Bina asked. "Ever since we came on board, you've never sat still. So why won't you help me now?"

I told Bina about my trip up top, and how they'd chased me out. "I escaped," I said, "but they were still looking for me. If they see me now, I'll be in trouble."

"Don't worry," she said. "It's a big ship. They have a lot of other work to keep them busy. They won't look for you."

Though I was still worried, this made sense, so I agreed to help her. I got some of the things for Jade's cage, and followed Bina. Some children we knew from the train followed us.

Up on deck Bina took Jade out of his cage. Bina said, "You never sit still," and the parrot repeated it over and over. "That's enough, Jade," said Bina. "I'm going to make you pretty."

"Pretty, pretty," he repeated.

The children laughed. I cleaned the cage thoroughly, and refreshed his drinking water and food, while Bina cut Jade's wings. As Bina tried to put Jade back in his cage, he bit her.

"You are naughty," she said. Holding him by his wings, she pushed him into the cage.

As the storm overtook us, Bhanumashi, who ran the garbas, got very sick, as did many other passengers. Bhanumashi couldn't move from her bed. "There will be no garba this evening," she said. The message spread from one person to another.

That night all we had was a movie. I brought a pillow, and others imitated me. The men at the movie laughed. "We thought you ladies would never get tired of the garbas," they sneered.

Some women ignored them, but one independent-minded woman named Kushum couldn't keep silent. She stood up. "What do you men know about us women?" she demanded, and it seemed as if an argument was inevitable.

But Tulsidas stopped them, saying: "Shut your mouths, all of you. The movie is starting."

The men apologized, while the other ladies insisted that Kushumben sit down. We watched a movie titled: "Neel Kamal." It was an intense love story with plenty of comedy, but it failed to keep our minds off the storm. The ship was rocking. The film caught in the projector, shaking the picture and marring the sound.

"What was that?" a woman asked.

"It's the storm," said a man coming down from the deck. "It's getting rougher."

I held Bina, then my hands went to my stomach and my mouth. "I can't hold it in," I said.

"Stand up and run to the bathroom," Bina told me.

"I can't," I said. "It's coming."

"Lay down," she said.

I lay holding my mouth with my little handkerchief. Things started shifting on the deck. Pots and pans banged against each other.

Tulsidas announced: "We will end the movie early... Now... Everyone go to your beds."

I wobbled to my berth.

The next morning the storm strengthened, and Donna's sickness intensified. She ran a fever, and she'd lost weight. I felt bad for her. She couldn't enjoy the journey. Though I felt hungry, I didn't dare put anything in my mouth. That afternoon, when the galley had already closed for lunch, teatime arrived. Mum insisted that I eat something with my tea. She gave me some leftovers. I ate a little, and was on my feet. I wanted to go up on deck. I needed fresh air.

"Don't go," a passenger warned me. "The storm is huge." I didn't listen. I needed to be out. Still wobbling, I walked up the stairs, holding onto the bars with every step. As I came on deck wind blew my hair over my face. I would have blown away, had I not gotten hold of a metal pipe. No one was up there but some crew members tightening ropes, and a few sailors who were asking all passengers to go back to their berths. Even the sailors were getting tossed around.

An angry sea rose up in monstrous waves, rocking the ship much harder. It felt as if the ship might capsize at any moment. Waves splashed over the deck. Anything that wasn't tied down would be swept away.

When I tried to get back to the stairs, the wind blew me back. I fell, and pain ran through my ankle and my hands. A sailor tried to help, but he was thrown across the deck. Somehow I managed to lift myself up, and get hold of a thick rope. I got back to the stairs, and slowly climbed back down. I was cold and wet. I changed out of my soaked clothes, wrapped myself in a blanket, and lay in bed.

A pregnant lady near us tried to go to the toilet. She slipped and fell on her back, crying: "It's coming! It's coming!" She tried to stand up but couldn't. Most of the passengers were in their beds. A few unaffected people played cards or chatted. With the roaring storm, they didn't hear the pregnant woman's cries.

She cried louder. She was afraid she'd lose her baby. Finally one of the crewmen heard her. He put down his broom and called out to her, "Miss, wait. I'll get help."

Other crewmembers arrived and carried her to bed. In her pain she could feel her baby moving. An older woman, who was experienced in home deliveries, calmed her down. This lady took command, ordering the other women to put up a bed sheet for privacy. Someone brought a bucket of hot water. They began sterilizing anything that needed to be clean. Someone else brought a handbook with instructions. The pregnant lady's screams came with her contractions. When the pain abated she said she wanted to be left alone. She was only seven months pregnant and did not want her baby born onboard the ship. She tried to hold in her baby. Her husband stood beside her, helpless. These men hadn't experienced a birth without their mothers there to guide them.

We were all anxious to hear the baby cry, but after four hours of agony the woman finally fell asleep. The pain seemed to be gone.

By the following day the storm was over. The damage on deck was minor, and easily repaired. After lunch, I took my book and sat at my favorite spot near the rails. I imagined our future life in India. Would the people be friendly? Would we like it there? Eventually I dozed off, but soon I was awakened by a quarrelsome voice.

I went to see what it was all about. A young woman was halfway up on to the railing. She had a dark look and was telling her husband she would jump overboard. This woman, who'd been raised in privileged circumstances, had been hearing troubling things about the hard life in India. She'd fallen in love with an Indian worker who'd been in Uganda on a contract job. She hadn't understood the details of his background. Part of this was due to his lies. He'd lied so that she would come with him, but now he had to tell the truth.

"I'm sorry," he told her. "I'll do my best to make you happy."

But she felt she could never adapt to life in an Indian village. Her father had opposed her marriage on these very grounds. Now she understood what he'd been saying. She wanted her husband to promise that they would live by themselves in a big town, and not with his family in a tiny village. Unless he could convince her that he would do this, she said she would throw herself into the ocean.

People tried to persuade her to come down. "Go get the Captain," one man told a boy.

The boy ran, shouting: "Captain, Captain! Come down!"

"What is it my boy?" the Captain asked.

"A lady wants to jump into the ocean."

The captain put his hat on and hurried down the stairs. He ran towards the crowd, but it was too late. This woman's leg slipped from the rails. She fell into the water. Her husband cried for help. Other voices joined his.

Some of the women started beating up the woman's husband. "Why did you lie?" they demanded.

"She didn't understand what she was doing," he said.

The captain ordered the engines to idle, and called in the deck officer. Sailors put on rescue vests. They lowered boats, and a few minutes later they had her back on board.

She was given CPR immediately. A doctor had been checking on her twice a day. The Captain called her onto the deck. We all prayed.

Luckily, she came back to her senses. "Good God," said an older man. "Look at these young couples. They're never satisfied. They fight for every single detail. In our time this did not exist. We got married and were happy with what we got."

I missed my afternoon tea.

The next day, Tulsidas announced: "This is your final dinner onboard."

It was a fine dinner. The two vegetables tasted even better with khadi sauce. We had gufi ice cream for dessert. Mum made friends with some people traveling to the same district where we were heading. She was glad. Now we could travel on the same train with people she knew. That way we would have good company, and everyone could watch each other's luggage. She recalled an India where things had been safer, but that had been thirteen years earlier. That made me wonder how she felt returning to her hometown. The last time she'd been to India she'd been with Papa, but now here she was, a mother alone with five children. It was a big responsibility.

After dinner, I sat on the deck, both my legs dangling over the water. This would be the last sunset onboard. I relaxed, and watched the sky turn red and yellow as the sun neared the horizon. I'd watched this every evening, and every evening it had been different. Every sunset had its own beauty. I sang to the sun as it dipped into the sea. Darkness fell everywhere.

As our escape from Amin came to a close, I began to realize that I'd learned a great deal. In a very short time I'd seen many different people living in ways that were entirely new to me. We'd helped each other, talked to each other, and laughed and played with each other. The next day we would reach India. All these people would travel their own paths, while doors would open, and I would meet entirely new people. I began to see that this was the journey of life.

But I was a normal young girl, not a philosopher, and not all of my thoughts were so profound. I overheard a couple of girls asking Bina if she would join them when they went to some clubs in Bombay. They said the sailors would be there. I wanted to go too, though I knew Mum would never allow it.

I had no idea how huge Bombay* was. When I thought of cities, I imagined Kampala, where we could walk anywhere, and be back home within a few hours. Bombay was an enormous, densely populated city. People could get kidnapped or lost, and disappear without a trace.

On that last evening the deck was full of people. Everyone was talking. There would be no more garbas on this voyage. My sisters and brother came to sit with me. We were anxious to see signs of land. We hoped for a few tiny lights that would grow bigger. Instead lights came, but then disappeared. Could they be crocodile eyes? I was sleepy, but I didn't want to go to bed. I wanted to have the very first sight of land, so I stayed out until midnight. Finally I slept for few hours, waking intermittently for a glance through the porthole, hoping for a sign of shore.

Our final day onboard was Saturday. At four in the morning I woke up my siblings, took a blanket and went

*The name "Bombay" was officially changed to "Mumbai" in 1995. In 1972 we knew it as "Bombay", so that is what I use here.

to sit on deck. Bina and Kevin came with me. It was cold and still dark. Only a few other passengers joined us. We looked into the darkness, and here and there we saw tiny lights on the water. We wondered if these were fishing boats, or could they be on shore?

Then at twenty-past-four on that Saturday morning, nine days after sailing from Africa, we saw land. There it was, far in the distance: Mother India. Lights dotted the coastline and the sky brightened, even though it was not yet sunrise.

"India!" I shouted.

Kevin raised his hands into the air, and pointed. "Look!" he cried. "There is land." He ran downstairs to tell Mum.

Mum was too busy gathering all our belongings. She wanted us to help. Bina went down below, but Kevin, Donna and I bundled ourselves in a single blanket, and watched the sunrise. We sat for hours gazing at the oncoming shoreline.

As we neared the shore I pointed to a huge flat slab, rising on some kind of big hinge, high in the air between the two shores of an inlet. "Look there," I said.

"It's a bridge," a man mumbled as he brushed his teeth.

I saw his rotten teeth and made a face, but then my gaze returned to the flat stone. "Wow," I said, "a bridge. I've never seen a bridge that big."

"It's a drawbridge," the man explained. "Once our ship passes through there, the bridge will come down to become a road."

"Wow!" I exclaimed. "India is great."

Down below Mum and the other passengers were already looking through the porthole. Everyone was getting excited.

At breakfast the cooks served us extra sweet dishes, thanking us for the help we'd given them throughout the voyage. We thanked them for cooking delicious food, and making our journey more pleasant. After breakfast, a group of us went back up on deck. We could see buildings now, and tiny moving dots that must be people. Though it was early morning, many Indians were already up, going through their daily routines.

The ship slowed as it neared the port. On reaching the harbor, our ship turned to the rear and waited.

Now we could see people who were close by. Men in their dhotis wore bead necklaces. Ladies by the water had their saris pulled from between their legs. This style was called "marathi sari." They bathed and performed their water ritual, holding water in their hands, before pouring it back into the sea. This rite of purification was accompanied by prayers to the Sun.

Mothers washed their children at the water's edge. Some brushed their teeth with green branches. This water didn't look at all clean, and I wondered how they could wash and brush their teeth in it. Mum said that these branches came from an antiseptic tree, but the whole process looked filthy. Unused to the customs of this culture, we could not help laughing.

Some of the ladies squatted near a big stone, washing clothes. They used the same dirty water. People climbed the stairs to a temple. They went in holding coconuts. Temple bells rang. The bells and the chanting of early morning Arti soothed me, making me feel at peace. Those sounds inspire me to this day.

I looked around, wanting to see as much as I could.

As the sun rose, the air got hotter and hotter. The hot wind smelled like overcooked potatoes—not a pleasant odor.

At eleven am the ship's horn sounded. We were nearing the harbor where we would dock. We dropped anchor at noon. They set up the gangplank, extending sections from both ship and shore.

As we disembarked we realized we weren't used to the incredible humidity of Bombay. Our throats were dry and we needed water. We each carried our belongings and walked together.

Some passengers touched Mother India's soil and asked a blessing as they first set foot on her shores. We lined up to have our passports stamped. As in Mombasa, we formed two long lines, but they moved much more slowly than they had in Africa.

"Why is it so slow?" I wondered.

"Welcome to India," said Kushummashi. "Here people work at their own pace. They don't care if you are baked standing in the sun. Look," she continued, pointing ahead at the line. "Here is a big line of people, all waiting to get their passports stamped. We have to do that before we all can go find rest after our long journey. But instead of stamping passports, these men are chit chatting."

I watched the men who were in charge of stamping the passports. Their mouths and teeth were horribly red, and their cheeks were swollen with whatever they were chewing. They mumbled every word, and you could barely understand them. This was because their mouths were full of beetle leaves. Every time one of these men stamped a passport he would spew his red spit against the wall behind him. I was amazed at their lack of manners.

How could they be so filthy?

India's government had decreed that we would all be treated with dignity, and be given food and drink. As we approached the tables the food looked yummy. It was North Indian cuisine: vegetables in gravy sauce, rice, naan, pickles and a sweet dish.

I loaded food on my plate, and we found seats on a nearby bench. I took one bite and jumped up. My whole mouth burned from spice. I asked for a glass of water. There was none. *What kind of a land have we come to?* I wondered.

Seeing one of the food workers, I asked: "Don't they drink water after lunch in this country?"

He nodded, saying nothing. Did his nod mean yes or no? I couldn't tell. I looked across the tables to the tea stand. There was no water to be found. One worker pointed, and I saw a tap. I ran to it, filled my cupped hands with water. It tasted bitter. I could only swallow a little of it. "What is this?" I mumbled. I felt like crying.

That was when Mum said: "Wait here at this bench. Do not go anywhere until I get back. I will check to see if our luggage arrived safely." It took her two hours.

When Mum returned we were totally parched by the heat, sun, and lack of water. We were glad to see her, but there was no sign of our luggage.

"You know what?" she said. "I saw all of our checked luggage and belongings behind the bars in the luggage room. I asked that they be released, but the customs officer denied my request. He said: 'Sister, come back tomorrow. Your luggage has not passed customs yet.'

"But now we must go to my sister's house. We will take

a taxi."

Mum gave a hand sign for a nearby taxi, but a rickshaw pulled up next to us. Pulling it was a skinny young man wearing pants, a loose shirt, and chewing a stick. His rickshaw was fully decorated. He had a photo of Lord Ganesh and garland in front of the steering column. Photos of movie stars were glued up on the sides of the back seat.

The Rickshawala, as they are called, snatched the suitcase from Bina's hand and put it at the back of his rickshaw. "Where can I take you?" he asked in Hindi.

"To hell," Mum snapped, pulling out the suitcase. "How do you think you are going to fit six of us, with all of our luggage in this little rickshaw? On your head?"

"Mamji," he said, "don't you worry. I will manage. Four of you can sit at the back with the luggage and two of you can sit next to me on one seat." Kevin quickly sat to the side of the driver's seat.

Mum pulled Kevin out. "We don't want to go anywhere," she told him. "Now you leave us alone." Mum's use of Hindi mixed with Gujarati surprised us.

The driver of the nearby taxi had been watching all this. Now he pulled up his cab, got out, and started putting our luggage in the trunk.

"Wait," said Mum. "Give me the rate to Andheri before you touch our luggage." At first he said nothing. "How much?" she demanded.

The driver gave her a rate that was triple what it should have been. He thought he could outwit these foreigners. Mum haggled until she got an acceptable fare, then four of us got in back, while Mum and Kevin took the front seat with the driver. With a great deal of honking, the taxi took off.

"Remember this," Mum told us. "You have to be harder to survive in this country."

Every car there honked all the time. There were no road restrictions or regulations. You had to drive carefully because the crowds of people spilled into the road. Cows stood in the middle of the road, unhindered. Some napped on the side, ignoring the traffic. The roadside was dirty, with trash thrown everywhere. The cows, which are holy and respected in India, scrounged for food in the trash near the market places.

Women were slapping clothes against stone walls, and dunking them in soapy water.

"What's that?" Donna asked.

"That's dhobi ghat," said the driver. "Washing people's clothing is the service they offer."

Donna laughed at this strange cleaning method.

The produce in the vegetable and fruit stalls was nicely arranged in neat piles with lights flashing on them. The sight of the tiny grapes made us even more thirsty. Shop doors and windows were covered with photos of famous movie stars. Big billboards advertised the most recent Hindi movies. Radios in every store and stall played Hindi songs. It was as lively and colorful a city as I'd ever seen.

I was surprised to see some men holding hands. These men were not gay. Most of the men wore bellbottoms that swept up dirt from the ground and pavement. Their shirts weren't tucked in, and they wore little scarves around their necks. From time to time they combed their hair back as they walked along.

"Wow, what a style," said Bina. We laughed. We soon learned men and women were not allowed to hold hands in public here in Bombay.

Policemen in their wide khaki shorts, had whistles hanging around their necks. They stood in kiosks at crossing points, directing traffic. When a rickshaw passed, the driver had to bribe these traffic police. Our driver told us this money went to a big boss somewhere.

It was painful to see skinny barefooted men pulling rickshaws full of passengers. These people had no luxuries. They were glad to earn a few rupees to feed their families and themselves.

At each stop sign, beggars, young kids and women with babies approached car windows, begging until they got some rupees. They would even get hold of moving cars.

"Keep your windows closed," Mum said.

"The children out there might be orphans, or they might have been kidnapped," our driver told us. "A big gang puts all of these people to work doing this. They'll cut off someone's leg, or pull out an eye, just to make the person a better beggar. Then each person must bring in so many rupees, or the gang beats them."

It was hard to see people in such poverty.

The main road was much nicer. We could breathe there. Some modern buildings stood along the roadside, and beside the buildings dogs, cows and wild ugly pigs searched for food amidst the dung.

Though we thought our driver was taking a shortcut, this was actually the longer route. We passed rows of little houses facing each other. Water gutters ran between the houses. Laundry hung out in front, and they shared common outdoor toilets. It looked filthy. Half naked children played in the dirt. Sun had bleached their dirty hair. The smell was horrible.

"It smells that way because it's been raining," said Mum.

We passed through a crooked pathway leading to an open area of retail shops. Mum told the driver to drive slowly. One of our uncles owned a shop here, and his house was behind his business.

Mum had the driver stop, and she showed the address to a shopkeeper. One of the shop workers called our uncle. Most people there knew him. Our uncle and aunty came out. They hugged us, remembering Bina and me when we were babies.

"Look how tall you have grown."

Uncle told his workers to bring our luggage into the small house. He haggled with the taxi driver, just as Mum had. Our uncle paid a fare that was slightly less than the one shown on the meter.

Our uncle and our mashi lived with their four little children in a two-bedroom house. Mashi had already cooked dinner and a sweet dish to welcome us.

Early the next morning Mum and Bina went to get our luggage. It was raining, and it took them all day. They arrived home that evening, but they were upset. Our bundle of blankets had disappeared. Mum suspected the customs people had stolen it.

"They were not friendly," said Mum. "They wanted money for the luggage they had there. They do this all the time here. They are all corrupt. I will have to go back tomorrow, but I won't pay them a single rupee."

On the third day she returned. She stood her ground, refusing to pay for what was already hers. Finally they gave her our luggage. Now that we had it, we were ready to take the eight- hour train ride to Gujarat.

Uncle and Mashi took us to the railway station in a

taxi. It was a madhouse of cars and taxis. At our uncle's direction, we monitored our luggage. Otherwise it might disappear.

Coolies in red dhotis and red turbans rushed to our taxi and started taking our luggage. Mum stopped them, and began negotiating the price to have our luggage taken to our seats. Of course, they wanted triple the normal rate. They picked up our luggage without asking and started walking away.

Our uncle took over the negotiations. Being a local helped. Soon he got a reasonable price from two coolies. I felt sad for them as they carried two suitcases on their heads, and our other bags at their sides. They rushed through the crowds, and we did our best to follow.

Uncle and Mashi went with us to the crowded platform. People from all over crowded there. Some carried their own luggage. Women from different places wore various types and colors of saris.

We children walked with the coolies while Mum was with Uncle and Aunty. It was so crowded that we had to push our way through the people to get onto the train. Finally we found our places. They put our luggage in front of our seats.

More than half of the train's first and second class was reserved for the passengers from Uganda, and we saw a lot of people from the ship. The train was a lot like the one we'd ridden in Uganda. First class passengers got air-conditioned private cabins with sleepers. The seats in second class were grouped into semi-private, six-seat sections, with upper, middle and lower berths. The lower berths became our seats during the day, converting to berths at night. Third class had wooden benches facing each other, with a top berth.

We said farewell to Uncle and Mashi, and took our seats. Uncle stayed even after the train started moving, but finally he jumped out. Mashi walked with the moving train, and Mum walked back through the car to keep her in sight. She and Mashi had a tearful farewell.

Finally we left the station. As we rolled through the suburbs of Bombay we couldn't seem to shake the bad smell. We saw people pooping on the railroad tracks. They carried small tin buckets of water which they used to wipe their butts.

Many local workers slept on the side of the road in small spaces near the buildings. Others slept in the tunnel. But the suburbs were more spread out and nicer. There were a few tall buildings, many small homes, and plenty of fields and lakes.

Every station was known for serving a special meal. All the platforms were jammed with passengers, coolies and beggars. There were always stalls selling tea and warm snacks, and sellers with food baskets on their heads walked through the train at every stop. They all repeated a word for whatever they were selling, calling it out over and over like a song. Little children with tea and water cans passed our windows, calling: "Chai, Pani." Beggars, mostly women with their half-naked babies, squeezed between them. They would not leave until we gave them some rupees.

At Surat station Mum bought specialty sweets that looked like spaghetti covered with ground nuts.

Ours was a special ladies reserved compartment with a guard. All the seats were already occupied by ladies, children, and construction workers. There was nowhere to stand or walk. The guard tried to push people out but failed. They wouldn't leave. I was sleeping on the top berth. I wanted to go to the toilet, but how would I get down? Could I just jump down and climb over them?

This was the Indian railway: another new experience.

The woman who'd threatened to jump off the ship was in a first class compartment. We heard that she had thrown up on her expensive sari after eating some spicy snacks from one of the stalls.

As we approached the Narmada River, Mum gave each of us coins. "You should throw this coin into the river to wish us good luck," she said.

I learned that the Narmada River was one of the seven most sacred rivers in India, Many wisdom and traditions around the world draw inspiration from rivers and their behaviors. This river was no exception. "Narmada" means "one who endows bliss." Every year, people from all over Gujarat come to take their ritual bath in its waters. After that came Vadodara station.

Mum got headaches the whole way. She hadn't had enough sleep, and she had to keep an eye on all our valuables.

"I will go get a nice cup of tea," she said to Bina and me. She knew tea would help her headache. "Watch our luggage." At the tea stand she was approached by Mr Soni from the African train. Though he had first class accommodations, robbers had entered his compartment while he was sleeping. They took his suitcase, passport and several important documents.

Mum offered him tea, and gave him our address. This made him feel a little better. The train was about to leave. "Mum!" we shouted. She left half of her tea, climbed aboard, and the train pulled out. Without her we would have had no idea where to go or what to do.

We ate the paratha Mashi had packed for us, then Mum gave us wet towels to wipe our faces. We brushed our teeth, put on face powder, and combed our hair, making sure we'd look pretty for our family—family we'd never met. Finally, at five in the morning, we arrived in the town of Anand. We were only fifteen minutes away from the place where we would start our new life.

***

Later we learned that Indians in Uganda were still being torched, harassed and killed. Many in higher posts weren't permitted to leave. Those who could were the fortunate ones. When the final deadline came, the UN's member nations sent many planes to Entebbe. There the last refugees, some stateless, were flown out of the country.

Papa was one of them.

One-and-a-half years later, we reunited with our father in Europe. When that happened, our flight from Idi Amin was finally over.

Acknowledgements:

A very special thank you to all my readers, all those who I've met on my life's journey, whose lives and experiences have helped me create this book. Sharing my story with you helped me realize just how important it is to surround myself with caring, supportive people. Creating this book helped me reconnect with my dear Ugandan neighbors, colleagues and friends. We have a lot of old memories to reminisce about, and it was wonderful to see "where we were and where we are now" and what we learned from our experiences.

To each and every one of my readers for letting me express my feelings.

To my parents for making me who I am today.

To my son, Amit, who unselfishly allowed me to hibernate so I could complete this project on time. Your sacrifices have not gone unnoticed.

To my daughter Renal for allowing me to see myself in her. You took care of one of the biggest roles, preparing most of your engagement and wedding plans: between your work, your spoiled dog D'jengo, your taking on-line classes for higher performance, and exams, giving me enough space to concentrate on my writing. You are an example to many. I am blessed to have had you come into my life.

To Dr Charleen Rocha, a dear part of my family, taking her time from her busy schedule to help me create a website for this book.

To my sisters and brother for giving me the wonderful memories.

To Jana Andres, a leadership coach and colleague who

helped me dig out my message for this book that lay deep within myself.

To a wonderful friend, Adassa, who I met six years back. Her serenity and radiating energy helped me understand that there is something greater beyond just the daily humdrum of human life. You're staying closer to my process since I started writing and creating a fun time at proof reading.

To Jeff Lamei. With his powerful healing knowledge, he helped me uncover and release the troubles that had pressured me. Through Jeff and Clara, a great spiritual Native American woman, I reconnected with my ancient Vedic knowledge. I see you as my mentor in my spiritual life.

To Linda Coleman. You and your book "For the Self-publishing Author" has been a great help to me in finding great ideas.

Many thanks to the country of Belgium, its generous people and the Caritas Catholica for their tremendous sympathy and support. This was the country that took my father as a refugee.

To Susie, Amber and Bonnie, my loyal employee's. You have been a great help in keeping my business stable during my absence. You ladies are awesome!

TIMELINE OF HISTORICAL EVENTS SURROUNDING
MY STORY:

The following is a chronological account of Ugandan history during that era, with special emphasis on the 1970s, Amin's seizure of power, and its aftermath.

1894 to 1962: Uganda is a British protectorate, which means it is a colony in the British Empire. During the early years of Uganda's colonial status, 32,000 workers from British India are brought into East Africa as indentured servants; most are there to help build the railroad. Many go back when the work is done, but some stay, often becoming professionals and merchants. They remain for generations.

1962: British rule comes to an end and Uganda becomes self-governing. It begins as a constitutional republic.

February, 1966: Prime Minister Milton Obote suspends the constitution, assuming dictatorial powers.

1967: Uganda's government puts a new constitution in place, once again proclaiming itself to be a republic, but giving all effective power to Obote.

January 25, 1971: Obote falls to a military coup led by Idi Amin Dada, known to the world simply as Idi Amin.

January, 1971 to August, 1972: Amin expands the army, while placing the country under military rule—meaning his rule. He encourages his army to terrorize and brutalize large parts of the population, including those of Indian descent. His "policy" is marked by numerous campaigns, and individual incidents of violence against "foreigners" and anyone he, or his forces, perceive as an opponent.

Early 1972: Amin's longtime animosity toward

Asians in Uganda begins to boil over. He calls them "bloodsuckers" and threatens them with violence and expulsion. Throughout these months there are many violent incidents, often fatal.

August 4, 1972: Amin announces that all people of Asian descent in Uganda must leave within 90 days. Though he later limits the expulsion to those who lack Ugandan citizenship, the effect is nearly the same: those whose roots are in the former British India must go within 90 days.

1973: By the end of this year, virtually all Asians have left Uganda. The few that are left have no influence or power.

1973-1979: Amin's reign is marked by further violence, most of it against Ugandans. Estimates of the death toll range from 100,000 to 500,000, with 300,000 being the figure cited most often.

1978-1979: Amin's forces attack Tanzania, but are repulsed by a combined force of Tanzanian army units and anti-Amin Ugandans. Though he gets aid from Libya, Amin's forces are driven back.

April 11, 1979: Opponents of Amin take over the Ugandan capital of Kampala. Amin and his allies flee to Libya. He spends the rest of his life in disgraced exile, first in Libya, then in Saudi Arabia. He never shows remorse.

2003: As Amin's health fails, one of his wives petitions Ugandan President Yoweri Museveni to let the former dictator return to his native land to die. Museveni replies that, whatever Amin's condition, the moment he sets foot on Ugandan soil he must "answer for his sins." Amin dies in Saudi Arabia on August 16, and is buried there.

Glossary:

Askari: Watchman

Antakshari: A Hindi movie song that begins with the Hindustani consonant on which the previous song ended.

Ashwin: Lunar month of September-October as per Hindu calendar.

Ayurvedic: A traditional system of treatments originating in Indian.

Ben, Bhai, kant,das, lal: Suffixes addressing men or women respectively.

Curfew: A regulation that requires all people to leave the streets at a prescribed hour.

Coolies: Porters.

Chai: Tea.

Djembe: Goblet-shaped drum.

Dussehra: Victory on the tenth-day of Navaratri.

Devshayani Ekadashi: The eleventh lunar day of the Hindu calendar. The month of June – July.

Dhanteras: Dhan means wealth and Teras means 13th day as per Hindu calendar.

Dhobi ghat: Laundry service.

Dhotis: Traditional men's garment worn in India.

Fango: a club-like tool with a sharp blade.

Ghee: Purified butter.

Gomesi: Traditional dress for women in Uganda.

Garbas: Gujarati folk dance played during the Navaratri festivals.

Gujarati: An Indian ethnic group that inhabits in the state of Gujarate.

Jape Mala: Prayer beads.

Kakwa tribe: An ethnic group of Nilotic origin residing in northwestern Uganda.

Kali Chaudas: The 14th day of Ashwin per Hindu calendar.

Kajal: Black eye liner.

Lugbara: The West Nile region in northwestern Uganda.

Langi and Acholi: Ethnic groups from central and Northern Uganda.

Makeko: Beach mats.

Mantra: A formula from the Veda chanted as an incantation.

Mashi: Terms of address for women by younger children.

Mangalsutra pendant: A wedding symbol given to the bride by husband.

Marathi: Indo-Aryan ethnic group that inhabits in the state of Maharashtra.

Navaratri: A nine day Hindu dance festival.

Nsenene: Grasshopper.

Ngoma: A cylinder-shaped drum.

Paratha: Spicy Indian bread.

Pani: Water.

Pritru puja: To feed the departed soul with food.

Puris: Small fried Indian flat bread.

Roti: Indian bread.

Rikshaw: Three-wheeled passenger cart.

Swahili: Language spoken in East Africa.

Surya Grahan: Solar Eclipse.

Tilak: A significant symbol for every married Hindu woman.